The Money Club

Jasmine Brown

Copyright © 2019

ISBN: 978-1-7342662-0-7

Cover design by Zoe Tikkun, Tyrone Robinson

Character Illustrations by Dominika Nowak "Nikadonna"

Edits by Ylonda Nichole & Vickie Couch

Book Editing by Kirsten Rees | MakeMeASuccess

Connect with Jasmine:

Instagram: @thejasmineamber | @_factsforyouth

Twitter: @_factsforyouth

Facebook: @factsforyouthnc

Email: info@factsforyouth.com

Website: www.factsforyouth.com

Disclaimer

The material contained in this book is intended for informational and educational purposes and will increase financial awareness. It is not intended for legal, accounting, or financial advice.

You are responsible for your own investments and financial decisions at your own discretion. Readers are encouraged to seek professional advice to make informed financial decisions.

The author is not responsible or liable for any financial gains or losses of any kind arising on account of any action taken pursuant to the interpretation of this book.

Acknowledgements

Having an idea and turning it into a book is as hard as it sounds. The experience is both challenging and rewarding. I especially want to thank the individuals that helped make this happen.

I have to start by thanking God. Without him none of this would have been possible.

My amazing parents, Rodney and Julie Brown. Although, we were going through tough times, this book gave me a way to put my feelings into something productive. I hope you see some good that came out of that time. Mom, you are the strongest woman I know and I'm proud I was able to be by your side during your fight. Dad, you're one of the biggest inspirations I have and watching you take care of the family during mom's fight showed me an even greater level of strength you possess. I didn't even know that was possible!

To my siblings, Raven, RJ, Jalen, Reagan, and my brother-in law Danny, you believed in me. Some days that was enough for me to write one more page or spend one more hour editing! Danny don't think I'm leaving out our argument…in a way that argument has led to the making of this book. I often had to describe it to remind myself the passion behind this project. FACTS!

To the Goon Squad. Christian, Ashley, Alexis and Ar'neka. You guys checked on me and encouraged me to keep going. You read chapters, gave suggestions, and were always supportive. Who could ask for better hype men!?

Josie, if you can believe it, this book is a direct result of the advice you gave me driving in the car in Malibu, CA. You sowed a seed in me that gave me the confidence I needed to start and finish this project.

Most of the characters drafted in this book, are based on people in my life whether current or past. Thank you to those that gave me character inspiration.

My team, well more like my person, Vianka. From reading early drafts, to giving me advice on the cover, to keeping me sane during the editing process, you played a vital role. This book wouldn't be finished without you. Thank you so much.

Contents

Money FACTS

84% of undergrads say they wish they had been taught more about money.[1]

Two-thirds of Americans can't pass a financial literacy test.[2]

The Center for Financial Literacy gave North Carolina a B-grade on teaching Financial Literacy.[3]

The Center for Financial Literacy has given five states a grade A, and those states are currently: Virginia, Utah, Missouri, Alabama, and Tennessee.[3]

In North Carolina High Schools, personal finances are taught in Civics and Economics class, but it has been found only 20 percent of the class covers finances.[4]

According to a 2019 survey by the National Foundation for Credit Counseling, 60% of adults continue to spend without a budget.[5]

---

[1] "Why Most High Schoolers Don't Know How to Manage Their Money." U.S. News & World Report. Accessed July 22, 2019.

[2] Farber, Madeline. "F-: Nearly Two-Thirds of Americans Can't Pass a Basic Test of Financial Literacy." Fortune. July 12, 2016. Accessed July 22, 2019. https://fortune.com/2016/07/12/financial-literacy/.

[3] "Is Your State Making the Grade?" National High School Financial Literacy Report: Making the Grade 2017 | Center for Financial Literacy. Accessed July 22, 2019.

[4] Wildstein, Eric, and Eric Wildstein. "Financial Literacy Could Become Graduation Requirement." Gaston Gazette. July 01, 2019. Accessed July 22, 2019.

[5] "2019 Consumer Financial Literacy Survey." NFCC. Accessed November 11, 2019. https://www.nfcc.org/2019-consumer-financial-literacy-survey/.

Ms. Brown
The Teacher

Chapter 1: The *Real World*

"Twenty pages!" someone shouts.

I look over and Brandon, the class clown, is glaring down at the study guide I had only just passed out.

"Brandon? Is everything okay?" I ask.

Silence whips around the classroom. All eyes are on him. He flips through the study guide, licking his index finger, grabbing the pages dramatically.

"I'm not doing this, Ms. Brown."

"Why don't you want to do the study guide?"

"Ms. Brown..." Brandon pauses. He shakes his head. "With all due respect, this study guide is trash. Math is trash."

"Excuse me?" I tilt my head.

My other students are whispering to each other. We're all waiting to hear the punchline to this joke.

"When am I going to use this in *real life?*" He folds his arms.

I'm shocked. Then I remind myself, he is a *kid*, trying to boost his social status, and get a reaction; I won't feed into his antics.

"You need to do this study guide to pass the midterm; it is *man-da-tory.*"

The class groans. They may not like it, but my message is clear.

"I am not going to use this in the real world," he insists.

I rub my temples, annoyed that this is still a conversation. I have been teaching here at Lakewood High for three years and, I'd never had a student refuse to do an assignment.

"Brandon, what makes you think that?" I ask, remaining calm.

"I'm not going to be an engineer, a doctor, a scientist, or a researcher..." Brandon rants as the rest of the class egg him on.

"Listen, you have to do the study guide for the midterm. It's part of your final grade to pass Algebra II. If you don't pass, you won't graduate." I glance around the room. "You guys want to graduate, *right?*"

A few kids understand, while the rest stare back at me with blank faces. I know many kids don't love math, but I try to teach the best I can. Most of my kids are sophomores, although I do have a few juniors and seniors who have previously failed. I feel as if I'm making a difference teaching; yet listening to Brandon makes me question if the curriculum is too hard, or if I am doing something wrong.

I scan the room: math problems are scribbled across the whiteboard; ungraded tests, quizzes, and classwork are piled high on my desk; and I have a colorful banner I bought at a thrift store on the back wall. It reads: "You can do it." I pull myself from my thoughts and back to the class.

"I'm going to work with my uncle in construction," says Brandon, "This is dumb..." He drops his pencil on his desk and leans back.

Now all eyes are on me, waiting for me to respond, and yet I'm stuck. As a teacher, shouldn't I have all the answers? Rebecca raises her hand.

"Yes?" I ask.

"No offense, Ms. Brown, I kind of agree," she says.

Brandon and Rebecca make eye contact.

I raise my eyebrows, trying to make sense of this rebellious attitude spreading through the class. Their shared feeling ripples around the entire room and it's written all over their faces! They think this study guide is pointless.

"Yeah, this is lame, I don't need this to ball," Jason chimes in, looking up from his phone. The whole class agrees in unison.

"Yeah, it might be lame, but it's *required*. And you *will* use it in the future."

"How, exactly?" Max, another one of my students asks. He looks back at the rest of the students from his front-row seat. "Look, I know for a fact my mom and dad don't use this algebra stuff at work."

Before the eruption of agreement gets out of hand, I speak up, defending my study guide.

"You will need algebra." I scramble looking for words. "For instance, when doing recipe conversions, figuring out a sales price, or when comparing interest rates for loans."

Rebecca shakes her head. Sean, who barely pays attention in my class, is engaged. That's surprising.

The class approval shifts to my side. I sigh, relieved.

"But math is trash!" Brandon whines.

"Okay, what about money? Is money trash?"

"No, we *need* money."

"Math *is* money." I see the class perk up.

"Where do we learn about money, Ms. Brown? Quadratic functions don't teach me anything about finance," someone yells.

"Quadratic functions may not—" I begin to say.

"Then what will?"

"There is a class called Personal Finance available to seniors if they choose."

"Nobody takes that class!"

"Yeah and I heard it's boring. The teacher sucks and all she does is use slides."

"It is an important elective to take." I smack my hands together.

"Yeah, if it's sooo important, why isn't it a requirement?"

The bell rings, preventing me from answering.

The students pack their bags and race out of class.

"Have a good weekend," I call out. No one says it back. Brandon's study guide is still on his desk. I shake my head disappointed.

I wonder, how am I meant to prepare my kids for their futures on a low teacher's salary and with a low budget. I already go above and beyond for my students. I am doing my job! I have spent over $200 in supplies. My classroom is at maximum capacity! What more do they need? I try to take my mind off things, yet Brandon's question pops up in my mind:

"When am I going to use this in the real world?"

It's on repeat.

Back when I was in high school, classes were smaller and teachers were paid better. I took Home Economics, which was an elective at the time. There wasn't a finance class offered then; I learned about finances from my dad. After all, he is a financial advisor. As I sit and reflect on my high school and college days, I realize, if it weren't for my dad and also my being a finance major in college, I wouldn't have the knowledge I do now.

It hits me: It's time to make a change.

I look at the time. Crap, there is a faculty meeting starting in a few minutes! I grab my tote and race out the door.

$ $ $ $ $ $

I slip in the back of the media center and sit next to Suzanne, who fills me in. Principal Matthews is going over new changes in the department. The debate with Brandon is still bothering me. As things wrap up, Principal Matthews opens the floor for comments and questions. I raise my hand.

Principal Matthews rubs his forehead. Maybe this wasn't a good idea. I clear my throat.

"I had an incident today, in my last class, involving some students. They think they aren't learning the right things to prepare them for the real world."

Principal Matthews gestures for me to continue.

"I think they are right. Our job is to prepare them, and we are dropping the ball."

I stop, hoping someone will say something but the room is silent.

"I think… we should teach them something tangible, things they can use in the future, like finances and…"

"We *are* doing our jobs. We are meeting state requirements."

I turn my head and see Mr. Davis. Of course, he would cut me off. We have had our quarrels in the past; he isn't too fond of me. He has always been polite, nevertheless everything I do, he has a problem with! He acts as if I am not qualified to teach at Lakewood. I have earned my stripes.

"It is not enough," I snap.

"I kind of see what you are saying, there just isn't enough time in the day to teach them the curriculum *and* real-world application," says Mrs. Green, shifting in her seat.

"Right, and we don't get paid enough…I agree with you, Ms. Brown, however, there's only so much we can do," says Suzanne.

"Suzanne, you are right." I pull my hair back. "Ms. Green, you are right, too, but who is responsible for teaching students how to survive as adults?"

I look at everyone and then at Principal Matthews hoping he would answer.

"It's the parents' job," Mr. Davis answers and it seems everyone agrees.

"What about the kids whose parents don't have the knowledge?"

Mr. Davis shrugs. No one says anything. I can see this is not going the direction I had hoped. It is beyond frustrating.

"If we continue to play this blame game, these kids will never be successful. It takes a village to raise a child, right?"

A few of the teachers agree with me. Mrs. Green turns in her chair to face me.

"You are right, however, these kids need to learn something at home. We can't do everything for them. We are not their mothers. We do too much and I don't see teachers' pay changing anytime soon," she adds.

I can tell the teachers are exhausted by this conversation and ready to go, but this is important.

"What do you suggest, Ms. Brown?" asks Principal Matthews.

"I think we need to teach a financial literacy course. It is the only subject I can think of that will help these kids."

Mr. Davis erupts with laughter. "You think these students are going to give a crap about financial literacy when they goof off in math?"

I glare at Mr. Davis. Doesn't he understand, even if they don't care about finances, we are setting them up for failure? We can teach them something important. I mean, does anyone care about these students beyond the classroom?

"Ms. Brown, doesn't Civics and Economics[6] cover topics like investment and savings?" Mrs. Green asks softly.

"I can tell you right now, the students are bored in that class."

"Because they don't care," Mr. Davis shouts.

"Everyone, calm down. This is a good discussion, let's not let it get out of hand," Principal Matthews says. He turns back to me. "What is your solution, Ms. Brown?"

---

[6] Personal Finance is only 20 percent of the class: Civics and Economics.

"Let's put aside time in or after class to cover the basics."

Suzanne sighs. "And who will do it? I can't...I'm too busy. I have my own kids at home to worry about."

Mr. Davis pipes up again. "Plus, these kids have bigger problems to worry about. Principal Matthews, I have kids who don't even know where their next meal is coming from. I got kids mixed in with the wrong crowd and hanging out with dropouts, and former classmates who are involved with gangs. These aren't small problems; we can't help them. Leave it to the parents."

I am shocked. Brandon is a child, but Mr. Davis? He is a grown man - a teacher. I can't believe he is acting like this.

"It's our job to prepare them for life after school. This is why I became a teacher in the first place!" I yell at him.

Mrs. Green puts her hand up, "Now. Ms. Brown-"

"No," I respond.

Mr. Davis hits the table, "Our job is to prepare them for the final to pass our class. They go to the next class and hopefully pass enough classes to graduate and leave here."

"What about Jason?" I ask quickly.

"What about him?" He raises his eyebrows.

"He reads on a third-grade level!" I throw my head back and laugh. This is unbelievable. I can't believe Mr. Davis.

"Jason is Lakewood's starting point guard, ESPN top recruit, Ms. Brown. He has a tutor," Mr. Davis retorts.

Before I blow up on him, Principal Matthews ends the argument.

"Okay, no need to bite each other's heads off. Ms. Brown, I can see your passion, but you know North Carolina has a B-grade in teaching financial literacy. Now, a B-grade is above passing. Personal Finance is built into the Civics and Economics course."

"Yes, Principal Matthews. But my students explained, no one takes the class, *or* takes it seriously, and I *know* Civics does not cover personal finances enough. It hasn't changed much since I was in school! We have to do better!!"

Mr. Davis groans. Mrs. Jones is preoccupied with her nails, Suzanne is on her phone, and the rest of the teachers look tired.

Principal Matthews takes a long breath. "Ms. Brown, once again, what is your solution?"

All eyes direct their attention to me. A dozen answers pop into my head. Who will teach these kids this stuff? I search for the right answer until I realize:

"The solution is me."

Chapter 2: The Great Idea

I head out from the meeting, making my way through traffic and stopping at Chick-fil-A to get some fries. I spend too much money eating out. I eat my fries as fast as I get them, head home, take a quick shower, and fire up my laptop. The blank word document stares at me, and I type:

The solution is me.

Why the heck did I say that? It sounded convincing when I told Principal Matthews I would teach the students financial literacy. I should have won an Oscar. I chuckle at myself while I sip hot tea. I wasn't faking, I believe I can help, but I'm no expert. I might have put too much pressure on myself. Oh well, I thrive under pressure - I think.

If things get too hectic, I can quit. Wait, tell Principal Matthews that Mr. Davis is right, the task is too much to handle? Not a chance. I have the entire weekend to come up with an afterschool proposal.

Of course, I couldn't teach finances during class. Maybe a club of some sort.

I get up from the kitchen table and plunge into the couch. I rub my temples, trying to spark an idea. I think the club after school will talk about money: managing, saving, spending, and investing it. I could ask my dad for help! Or better yet, maybe he can talk to the club, like a special guest or something. Yeah, great idea. I spring up from the sofa and hunch over my laptop. I type:

Mr. Brown, special guest: financial advisor - he will talk about investing, interest, etc.

I smile, not a bad idea. I wonder who else I could bring to class. Ooh, I can ask some of my friends from college if they can speak! Ideas are hitting me fast.

Let's see, club meetings will be twice a week, Tuesday and Thursday from 3:00 pm to 4:15 pm. Special guest every club meeting: An athlete, someone who works in a bank, a business professional, a school counselor maybe?

Okay, okay, okay. Things are sounding pretty good. The Money Club should be a hit. I pause in the middle of typing. The Money Club...sounds pretty good. I say it out loud. *THE MONEY CLUB*. It sounds *really* good. I type it:

The Money Club

Excellent! I say it again a few more times to make sure it clicks. It does! Principal Matthews is going to be thrilled, how could he not? I open up my Gmail and prepare *The Money Club* proposal.

All I need is thirty days and two meetings a week. Thirty days to prove to Lakewood I can do it. I finish typing up the proposal and click send. I take out my phone. It is a quarter 'til 3 and I'm tired, but finally satisfied. I take a deep breath and tell myself I can do this. I can make *The Money Club* work.

$ $ $ $ $ $

It's the first day of *The Money Club* and I'm so nervous. I can't shake Mr. Davis' *"positive words of encouragement"* ...not even hot tea or yoga could shake away that kind of negativity. Brandon's tantrum three weeks ago has been on my mind every day since. All the pressure has been building and I can't help but think some people want to see *The Money Club* fail. Of course, I have support from a few teachers, but who I really need support from is Principal Matthews. His email response to the syllabus I drafted was dry:

Ms. Brown,

It seems The Money Club will take a lot of work to organize in a few weeks. Nevertheless, I admire your ambition. Hopefully, some students will come.

With optimism,

Matthew Johnson
Principal
Lakewood HS

I honestly didn't know how to respond to that. I can't get mad at what people don't understand and I don't have time to worry about Principal Matthews. Like my dad says, "We have bigger fish to fry." To be wise is to know what is needed and take heed.

You would think I had swim practice this morning, I'm at school at 6 am. The only teacher here is coach G; he loves his morning workout. I catch him outside of the weight room and gave him the whole *Money Club* spiel.

It is crazy how he saw value in *The Money Club,* and he teaches gym and coaches football! I even convinced him to make some of his players come to the club this afternoon. Yes, there will be more students than Principal Matthews thinks. I whip my phone out and check my To-Do list. I have a few more tasks to get done before the start of my first class. And the hardest of them all?

Get Brandon to come to Day 1.

Brandon
The Athletic Class Clown

Chapter 3: Just Another Day at Lakewood

I look at the sausage biscuit, grab it, and run out of the store. Sweat pours down my face as I race through the parking lot, searching for Jason's Honda Civic. My heart is beating extra loud. I can still hear the cashier yelling at me. It wasn't my plan to take the biscuit. I spot the Honda. I look over my shoulder one last time. The coast is clear.

"Jase, open up!" I knock on his car door.

The door unlocks. I scoot in the passenger side, panting.

"Why were you running?"

I take out the sandwich and gobble it down. Jason shakes his head.

"It's not what you think," I say, stuffing my face with sausage.

I wait for Jason to say something as I cram the wrapper in my pocket. The biscuit was small, not enough to satisfy the pit in my stomach.

"You could have come to my house, you know."

I didn't answer.

"We had pancakes." Jason turns on Lakewood street.

"Sounds nice."

I *was* hungry, but I didn't want to go to Jason's parents' house. I'm not a freeloader. My mom has been working two full-time jobs to provide. It is enough to put a roof over our heads, just not enough to stock the fridge. Last night wasn't the first time it was empty, and it wouldn't be the last. I am tired of eating instant ramen.

Jason shrugs. I put my headphones in my ear and turn my music up. I regret not taking Jason up on his offer to eat at his house. I know when I get home there won't be any food. I got too much on my mind and not enough on my plate.

We pull up to Lakewood High. My favorite place in the world. Jason parks in the student section. I get out of the car. He stays to wait on Mike and Bryan. I give him a nod and leave.

$ $ $ $ $ $

My first class is History. I like it because Mr. Johnson lets me sleep. The only class I'm going to have a problem with is math, good ole' Ms. Brown. Man, she's something. Last week, I refused to do her stupid study guide, and now she's doing some money club thing after school. Teachers are so extra! I haven't even done my packet. It's pointless. I can do it; I'm not dumb. I could have a 5.0 if I wanted to. But what's the point? I'm not going to college to get some fancy degree.

I get to History. I dap up a few of my teammates. I wave at Mr. Johnson, put my head on the desk and drift off.

I don't remember much from History class. All I remember is I slept great. I don't know what we were watching; I think a documentary on a war or something.

After History, I have Wood Shop, an easy A. I love building stuff, and Mr. Frank is the coolest teacher at Lakewood. After Shop, it's lunch and then my two worst subjects, science and math. Mrs. Green and Ms. Brown ask me to do way too much.

In Science, Mrs. Green's lips were moving, but I have no idea what she was saying. We were supposed to be doing some lab on rock-soil, I don't know. I was on IG all period. I leave Biology without my homework, like I always do, and head to Algebra II. I get to class and sit down next to Rebecca. Jason comes in and we smack hands.

"What's up, fam."

"What up."

Jason looks at me.

"What man?"

Jason lowers his voice, "Y'all, gonna do that study guide?"

I fold my arms and lean back in my chair and chuckle.

"It's not hard," Rebecca rolls her eyes.

"No, I'm not doing it," I reply.

"You a fool," Jason cracks up and plops right next to me.

The rest of the class comes in, including Ms. Brown whose eyebrows are standing on the top of her head. I bet she is going to give us another study guide.

Ms. Brown walks to the center of the class.

"Today's the day!" Ms. Brown exclaims, as she walks up and down the aisles.

No one says anything.

"You guys aren't excited? It's the first day of *The Money Club*. You will be learning about real-world topics!"

Ms. Brown clasps her hands together, waiting for us to reply. One of her eyebrows lowers.

I raise my hand.

"Will we get extra credit?"

"Yes, everyone who attends will get extra credit for one class assignment and two test grades."

I drop my mouth open. You got to be kidding me.

"Are you coming, Brandon?" Ms. Brown asks me.

"Duh, he is coming," Rebecca adds.

I laugh along with everybody. I need them test grades. I ain't got nothing else to do.

"Ms. Brown, what is *The Money Club* all about? Are we going to be doing math stuff?" Rebecca asks.

Ms. Brown turns towards Rebecca.

"*The Money Club* will be about personal finances." Ms. Brown grabs an eraser from her desk and wipes the board clean.

"Okay. What are we going to be doing?"

"You will be learning about things like saving and budgeting. All things you need to know to be financially stable in the *real world*." Ms. Brown cuts me a look.

"What?" I put my hands up like I'm innocent.

"Brandon, I hope to see you there." Ms. Brown points at me.

Everybody laughs.

$ $ $ $ $ $

The bell rings. I rush out of class as everyone pours into the crowded hallways. Today wasn't too bad for a Tuesday. I want to stop by Coach's office and talk to him about postseason workouts, but I won't have time if I want to go to this money club thing. I send Jason a text. If he goes to *The Money Club*, I'll go.

Me: Jason you going to the money club thing today?

Jason: Yea coach C is making me

Me: That's crazyyyyy

Jason: IKR

Me: Where you at

Jason: With becca :)

Me: Ah shoot

Jason: Nah we in ms browns class

Me: That's where the club is at

Jason: Yea.

Me: Bet

Me: What time do it start?

Jason: 5 mins

Jason: You coming????

Me: Maybe...

Jason: Bet

Welp, looks like I will go to the club. For some reason, I'm nervous. I knock on the door. I can hear some woman's voice. It sounds like an older lady. I open the door and see a woman smiling at me.

"Nice of you to join us," the lady says.

Behind her, I see Ms. Brown also smiling at me from her desk. There were some students I have never seen before. I sit next to Jason and Rebecca. My nerves ease a little. There are about twelve students here. I'm not sure who this big lady is; she dresses too professional to be a teacher.

Chapter 4: You Can Bank On It

The lady smiles.

"Hello everyone, my name is Mrs. Lawrence. I am a banker at the Credit Union here in Lakewood. I have been working there for fifteen years. I see and help different people every day with their checking and savings accounts. Does anyone here have a personal bank account?"

She looks around the class like she's a health inspector.

No one raises their hand.

"What about your parents? Do they own a bank account?"

I see a few hands go up.

"Good, good." Mrs. Lawrence smiles again. "Where do you guys keep your money safe then? A book bag? Wallet? Shoebox? What about in your dresser? Under your mattress?" Mrs. Lawrence stands, waiting for an answer.

Some of us raise our hands.

"Go ahead, no need to raise your hands, this isn't class."

"I keep my cash in my wallet," I say.

"In my purse," says a girl from behind me. I look. I didn't recognize her. She might be a freshman.

"Anyone else?" Mrs. Lawrence asks.

"I keep all my extra change in a Mason Jar," another guy says.

"Okay." Mrs. Lawrence points at some freshman in the front who had their hand raised.

"Where do you keep your money?"

"I save it in a jewelry box my grandmother gave me."

"Oh okay, I see. Do you think the jewelry box is a safe place?"

"Yeah."

"What if someone stole it? What would you do?"

She shrugs.

"I'd beat their a—" I butt in.

Everyone laughs. Jason gives me a high five.

Mrs. Lawrence chuckles. "Well, what if you kept your money in your house and your house burns down, or a tornado rips through it. Insurance might cover it, but...what if you don't have insurance? Then what would you do?" Mrs. Lawrence rocks back and forth on her heels waiting for an answer.

Dang, Mrs. Lawrence didn't have to go to the worst-case scenario. She extra too, SMH.

No one says anything again. I mean, I don't know what to say, I keep most of my money in a wallet, the rest is at home in my Nike shoebox and my mom has a jar she saves coins in.

"If you lose your money, you cannot replace it," Mrs. Lawrence cuts the silence. "Also, if you save your money at home, it cannot grow. If you put your money in a bank, your money will be secure and accumulate. I'm going to give you my six reasons all teens should open up a bank account."

6 REASONS WHY YOU NEED A BANK ACCOUNT

6

1) **LOW OPENING DEPOSITS**

2) SAFER

3) **NO MONTHLY MAINTENANCE FEES**

4) START SAVING EARLY

5) **STEPPING STONE TO GREAT CREDIT**

6) EASY

[7]

---

[7] Higuera, Valencia. "7 Reasons Why You Need to Open a Student Bank Account ..." Allwomenstalk, October 8, 2014. https://teen.allwomenstalk.com/reasons-why-you-need-to-open-a-student-bank-account/.

"Does everyone have a pencil and paper? I would take notes."

Crap, I didn't bring paper with me. I look up and there is Ms. Brown in front of me handing me a paper and pencil. I whisper thanks and begin copying from the board. Mrs. Lawrence says the credit union, among other banks, has low opening deposits.

She goes on about the reasons we should all have bank accounts and then tells us about the different types of accounts.

- <u>Savings Account:</u> an account at a bank that accumulates interest

- <u>Checking Account:</u> a personal bank account which you can take money out of at any time using your checkbook or bank card; it also accumulates interest.

I don't have a savings account. I don't even think my mom has one.

"Think of saving as giving yourself a reward," says Mrs. Lawrence and takes a swig of water. "People save money for things like buying a car, a down payment for a house, and for college. Keep in mind, you won't be able to save for something big overnight." She smiles. "You guys are young, so take advantage! Go to the bank and open a savings account."

"Accumulating interest is a perk for bank accounts. You can't get interest from saving money in a shoebox or piggy bank. The amount of interest depends on what type of account you open. The average interest of savings accounts is around .22 percent."

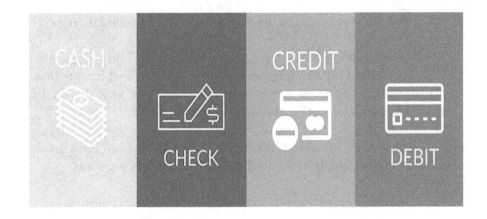

"Okay, here are four traditional ways to pay." Mrs. Lawrence points at the slide. "Cash is the most liquid option. A 'liquid' form of money or 'liquidity' means how fast something can be turned into cash[8]. Cash is an easy and fast option, but there are no security measures with cash. If one of you drops twenty dollars on the ground, it would be hard to track who the twenty belongs to."

Debit cards:

- debit cards are like plastic cash, they are more secure than cash.

- debit cards link directly to your checking account

- requires your name, signature, and sometimes a picture

-you can get notifications from your bank about your account via text or email

"Unlike with cash, if you lose your debit card, you can deactivate it preventing anyone from accessing your money. Once you lose a twenty-dollar bill, chances are it's gone forever."

---

[8] Mueller, Jim. "Learn about Financial Liquidity." Investopedia. Investopedia, July 14, 2019. https://www.investopedia.com/articles/basics/07/liquidity.asp.

"Right," we all echo in unison.

"Mrs. Lawrence, I don't use cash, I use Cash App. It is mad easy," says Max.

"Right, I use Cash App too," I say, waving a hand.

"True, you can use Cash App or Zelle," Ms. Brown responds. "There is also Samsung and Apple Pay. One of these days, cash will be a thing of the past."

"Right, although before you can use these apps you must have a bank account and a debit card linked," Mrs. Lawrence shares.

"Wow, another reason why you should get a bank account!" Ms. Brown reminds us.

Mrs. Lawrence claps her hands together. "Okay, the next way to pay, is a credit card. With a credit card, you are borrowing money that you do not own and will have to pay back with interest."

I jot this down.

"The last way to pay is with a check. I am old! Back in my day, we used checks way more than you guys do now. However, you still need to learn how to write one. You never know when you'll need to use a check to pay for something." Mrs. Lawrence pauses. "You guys are still taking notes, right?"

Checks - use a check for some businesses, gift-giving, and utility bills [9]

"Now, let's learn how to write them."

---

[9] "Why You Still Need Paper Checks and How to Use Them Safely." Money Crashers, June 6, 2019. https://www.moneycrashers.com/why-need-paper-checks-use-safely/.

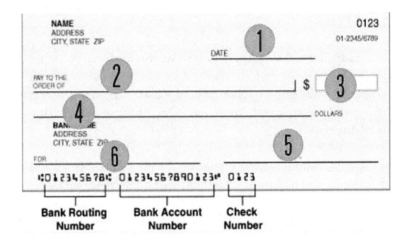

HOW TO WRITE A CHECK

1) CURRENT DATE
2) PAYEE
3) AMOUNT IN NUMERIC FORM
4) AMOUNT IN WORD FORM
5) SIGNATURE
6) MEMO OR "FOR" LINE

[10]

---

[10] "How To Write A Check: Teens Guide To Money: Teens Guide To Money." How To Write A Check | Teens Guide To Money | Teens Guide To Money. Accessed September 12, 2019.

"Okay guys, this is a blank check. I want you guys to use this format to practice writing your own. Ms. Brown and I will be passing them out. FYI, they aren't real."

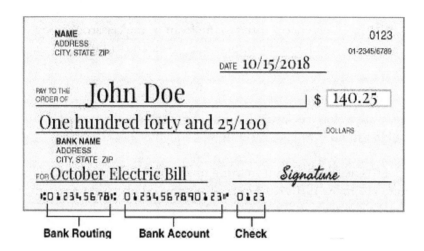

Mrs. Lawrence and Ms. Brown pass out blank checks to everyone and give us a couple of minutes to practice. I follow the example, and I lay my signature on thick. Jason checks over it. We smack hands. I know my signature is on point.

"Time's up! How did everyone do with writing their own checks?" Ms. Brown and Mrs. Lawrence walk around the classroom, both taking a look at our checks. Mrs. Lawrence stops at my desk.

"Hmm, nice signature," she says.

"Well you know, I have been practicing in case I get famous."

---

http://www.teensguidetomoney.com/saving/checking-account-basics/how-to-write-a-check/.

Mrs. Lawrence looks at Jason's and Rebecca's signature. She smiles at them. Ms. Brown checks on the students behind me, and Mrs. Lawrence tackles the rest of the students.

"Nice work, you guys." She gives us a thumbs-up.

Mrs. Lawrence returns to the front of the classroom. She looks at her watch. I pull out my phone, too, to catch the time:

4:15 pm

The club has lasted for an hour so far. To be honest, I wouldn't mind if today's meeting was longer.

"Last thing I want to bring up is how to choose the right bank. There are many different kinds of banks and choosing the right one can take some effort."

CHOOSING THE RIGHT BANK

1)Check for fees

Checking account, Overdraft, minimum balance

2)Accessibility

ATMs or branches within walking/driving distance

3)Online Access

Online bill pay/money transfer

4)Safety

Insured by the FDIC or NCUA [11]

---

[11] https://www.nerdwallet.com/blog/banking/how-to-choose-a-bank/

I write while Mrs. Lawrence is talking:

<u>Checking account fee</u>

    - Sometimes there is a fee to open an account.
    - Can be as low as $0.

<u>Overdraft fee</u>

    - Fee if you spend more than you have (your account reaches a negative balance)

<u>Minimum amount fee</u>

    - If your account goes below a certain dollar amount.

"Next, make sure your bank is accessible: in driving distance and or has online access."

"Facts," I call out. "And an app!"

"I know that's right," a freshman calls out.

"Mrs. Lawrence?" I ask.

"Yes?"

"What do F-D-I-C and N-C-U-A mean?"

"It's a third party who insures the bank[12]," Mrs. Lawrence answers.

"Gotcha."

Mrs. Lawrence wraps things up and we all finish writing our notes. I don't even know the last time I wrote notes in a class!

---

[12] "Federal Deposit Insurance Corporation." FDIC. Accessed September 12, 2019. https://www.fdic.gov/about/learn/symbol/index.html.

Mrs. Lawrence says goodbye, and Ms. Brown ends the meeting. I'm already thinking about putting all the money I have into a savings account. I don't know. Everything Mrs. Lawrence said floats around in my head. Bank accounts...writing a check...maybe I'll come to the rest of the sessions.

My stomach rumbles.

"You coming for dinner?" Jason asks, while walking out to the car. "My mom's cooking spaghetti."

I think about it for a second.

"Can't turn down an offer like that!"

"FACTS."

Sean
The Skater

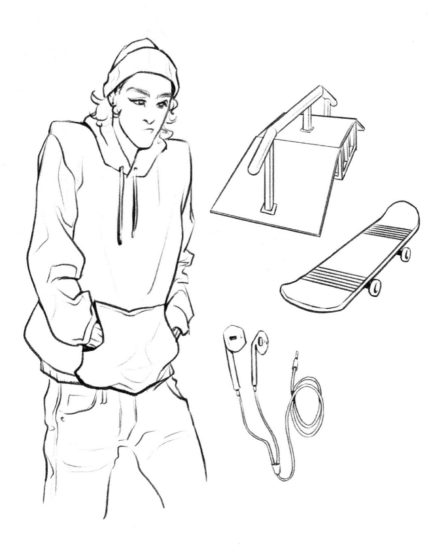

Chapter 6: *Parents Just Don't Understand*

My mom pretends to listen to me as I tell her about this study guide for math. She nods, sips her coffee, and continues to look through her phone; I know her mind is on her job. She is a neonatal surgeon, works long hours, and rarely has time for anything.

"What do you think?" I ask her to make sure she is listening. I ask her again.

Instead of answering, she stares at her iPhone scrolling.

"Mom!" I yell.

She snaps out of her daze and looks up at me confused.

"Oh, I'm sorry honey." She scrunches up her face. "What were you saying again?"

"Un-freaking-believable." I put my head in my hands.

"What? I'm sorry."

"Mom, it would be nice if we could have a decent conversation this time instead of hi and bye."

I shake my head. Both of my parents work at the hospital; my dad is a physician in the ER. Having two parents who are doctors is frustrating. I basically take care of myself.

"Sean, I am so sorry, it has been a busy week." My mom sighs in between taking sips of coffee.

Honestly, I could have told her I got drunk last night and she wouldn't flinch. I grab the lunch I packed from the counter. Still, I tell my mom I need lunch money; she points to her purse. I take a couple of twenties she won't miss and put them next to the wad of cash I already have in my back pocket.

As I head to the bus stop, I have the urge to skip school. I don't think my parents would even know. I would rather be skateboarding downtown...anything. My mom says *I need to go to school and get good grades to be a doctor.*

What if I don't want to be a doctor? Have they ever thought about that! I want to become a professional skater, maybe even open my own skate shop or something. *Anything* but a doctor. Every time I tell them what I want to do, they brush it off like I'm going through a phase or something. My grandfather was a doctor, my grandmother was a nurse. That isn't my destiny, I'm a skater, that is who I am.

I get on the bus for school, take my phone out, and post some pictures of me skating at "The Hill" on Instagram. I have a ton of followers already. I get love from people all over the world. I don't skate to be cool: I skate to be great. I spend the rest of the trip scrolling my feed. It doesn't take too long for us to arrive at this dump.

Ladies and gentlemen, welcome to Lakewood High, the suckiest place on earth. The cafeteria is full. I avoid crowds like the plague. Crowds are way too noisy, and everybody here follows the trends. Sometimes, I go to the bathroom or meet up with some of the guys I skate with. I don't have too many friends here; most of my friends are online and from Fortnight.

First period, I'm stuck in Biology. We're watching a movie about rocks. Second period, I have U.S. History. I don't mind it. I actually do pay attention in this class. Mrs. Davenport is old as heck. She might be older than Mr. Davis, but hey, she knows her stuff and you can tell she's passionate about teaching. I respect teachers like that.

My third class is Art and Design. No, I am not talking about drawing and painting, it is a computer class. It would be dope, but most of the kids surf YouTube and mess around. This is the only class I have an A in; not too shabby huh?

My last class is Algebra. Taught by none other than my "favorite" teacher, Ms. Brown. I don't know what has gotten into her lately; she has been pressing this money club thing hard.

She hasn't got me to care about Algebra, yet somehow, she has convinced me to stay after for *The Money Club*. By "convinced me," I mean I need this extra credit, seriously. Like Brandon, I didn't do my study guide. I don't agree with everything Brandon says, but he is right about this. I don't want to go to college; I want to move to Cali and skate.

I don't see what high school is doing for me. On the other hand, I need these classes to graduate. Plus, I don't want to be at Lakewood longer than I have to be. A diploma equals a job. I know if you don't graduate high school it's hard to get a job. My parents tell me that all the time, but what is the point of graduating if I'm not learning anything? That is the only reason I'm going to *The Money Club* today.

I shift around in my seat. Ms. Brown is at her desk, buried in paperwork. Class ended thirty minutes ago. I don't think I have ever stayed at Lakewood after school. I check my phone and the time. Yes! I got a new follower. I check their page scrolling through, double-tapping their photos. One thing I found out about IG is showing love and hashtags is the best way to build your followers up. I use social media to brand myself.

I look up from my phone. Dang, the class is full now. I shove my phone into my pocket. Ms. Brown is standing next to some tall nerdy guy with a plaid shirt and black glasses. This will be interesting.

$ $ $ $ $ $

"Hey everybody, Welcome to day two of *The Money Club*!" Ms. Brown starts clapping.

Yay, I mouth. This is going to be so boring.

"I have a special guest for you guys, today. This is Kyle," Ms. Brown points at him. He comes forward, smiling almost as hard as Ms. Brown.

"Hello," Kyle waves at us.

We echo hello back.

"My name is Kyle, and I recruit employees for BlackHat. I'm going to talk to you guys about money management, jobs, and entrepreneurship."

I lean back in my seat. This might be pretty chill.

Kyle clears his throat. "Often, we already know what we want to spend our money on way before we get paid or even have a job. After we get paid, we spend money on things we don't need. When we do, we tend to spend more." Kyle paces back and forth across the front of the room. "What do you buy with your money? Do you spend your money on wants or needs? First, can someone tell me what a want is?" Kyle looks around.

Max raises his hand. "It's like a desire or something you really, really want."

"Right, what are some things you guys want?"

"I want a girl to love me even when I'm low, Mr. Kyle," Jason cuts in.

Everyone erupts with laughter.

"I get it, I get it. Okay, what else?"

"I want a new skateboard," I say.

"What kind?"

"I have been eyeing this new skateboard that just came out."

"Nice. It's okay to want the newest skateboard, but a want is not a necessity. You can live without it."

"What about a phone?" Max asks.

"A phone is sort of tricky, no one really needs an iPhone."

"Shoot...I needs that," yells Brandon. I nod my head.

You can do anything and everything with iPhone. I mean without my phone, how could I function?

"A phone isn't a need because it isn't a basic necessity. Needs are like food, shelter, and water."

"What about a backpack?" Max asks.

Kyle smiles, "Yeah, items like a backpack for school, toilet paper, or glasses to see can be classified as a need. Now if you see a designer bag, that isn't a need."

"I guess I see what you are saying…"

"Now we know what a want is! It can get confusing, I know. Let me break it down for you guys."

"Here are examples of different wants and needs. On the left side, we have shelter, clothes, and food which you can't live without. And on the right side, we have wants. Like expensive cars, movies and concert tickets, even your daily Starbucks latte, Ms. Brown."

Ms. Brown laughs from her desk.

"Yes, I am guilty, I love my coffee." Ms. Brown raises her cup.

A few people laugh.

"Spending money on wants and needs can cause you to overspend. Overspending keeps you away from your financial goals. Does anybody have financial goals?"

"What do you mean?"

"Are you saving your money for something special?"

"Oooooh, Mr. Kyle, I think I understand what you are saying, I stopped buying stuff to get this." The curly hair girl takes out a shiny new iPhone from her bag, "I bought it myself. My parents said they couldn't afford it or whatever, so... I decided to get a job."

"That is a good example. So, did you have to make other money sacrifices to buy your iPhone?"

She scrunches her face, "What do you mean?"

"Like, did you skip out on the movies or other things you wanted to buy the phone?"

"Oh yeah, I had to make sacrifices! I decided to skip out on a concert with my friends over the summer to save up. I was bummed, but I was like the first person to get the new iPhone."

"Great, what is your name?"

"Maria."

"Thanks, Maria for doing the work for me! That is the next topic, financial goals!"

SMART: Goal Setting
Strategy

Specific

Measurable

Achievable

Relevant

Timely

"There are going to be things you want to buy or need to save for, like college or a car. You need to develop smart goal-setting strategies[13] to be able to afford what you want. But first, you need an income. For example, Maria got a job."

Maria's smile widens.

"So, Maria, how long have you been working at your-"

"I work in my neighborhood as a lifeguard over the summer, and then during school, I work part-time at the YMCA." Maria beams.

"How long did it take you to buy this new iPhone-"

"It took me five months. I worked hard," Maria rubs her phone case. "I kind of like it better that I bought it myself."

"Okay, Ms. Independent." Brandon smirks.

A few people in the class snicker.

Maria rolls her eyes at Brandon.

"Independent is good. What Maria is doing is preparing herself for the 'real world'."

"Working at your age is a good thing," Mr. Kyle begins. "It gives you connections and tells someone like me, who may be recruiting for a role, that you have experience. I started working when I was seventeen and I have a great job now, and I didn't go to college."

"Wait, what do you do again?"

"I am a job recruiter."

---

[13] "Developing Smart Goals" Walden University Academic Skills Center "PDF," 2017.

I can't tell you how many times I have heard the spiel of how important college is from everyone in this school. And here I am listening to a guy who looks rich talk about how he didn't even go to college. I wish my mom could see this.

"I tried to tell y'all we didn't need to go to college," Brandon yells.

Jason shouts, "FACTS!"

"You don't always need college, but you might need something like a certification or a trade. I like working with people. I followed my passion and made it into something real. But I never would have followed it, if I hadn't gotten a job in the summer of my sophomore year. My summer job made way for an internship. That internship got me in the door. My work ethic got me the job."

Wow, Kyle knows what's up.

"Anybody else here work?" Mr. Kyle asks.

Three other people raise their hands.

Kyle calls on one of the girls who had her hand raised.

"I work at The Wood Cinemas on the weekends, and over the summer I work full-time," she says.

"Are you saving your money?"

"Not yet, but I will after this club meeting."

We laugh.

"For the rest of you who didn't raise their hands, would you guys consider getting a job?" Mr. Kyle asks.

Jason shakes his head, Brandon and Rebecca do too, and some other kids mumble.

"I know a first-time job can be nerve-wracking. You may not know where to work or even how to fill out an application; but trust me it is easy. There are plenty of jobs a high school student can get."

As Mr. Kyle is talking, I write some of his examples down. At this point, I'm thinking a job might be a good idea.

- *Grocery store:*
  - *Food mart, farmer's market*
- *Jobs at the mall*
  - *Food court or apparel store*
- *Restaurants*
  - *Coffee shop, waiter, fast food joint, pizza shop*
- *Summer jobs*
  - *Book store, lifeguard, summer camp*

I think I would do best working at an apparel store. Maybe I can work in the mall or at a skate shop! That would be dope. I underline some of the places where I feel like I could work. Mr. Kyle describes the application process: what to wear for your job interview and how to impress them.

"Alright, now let's talk about something seemingly tricky, your W-4."

"Huh," Brandon says and I shake my head.

I'm confused. Way too many words.

"Yo, what the heck is that? My brain hurts," Jason calls out.

"Me too, fam."

Mr. Kyle and Ms. Brown laugh.

Form W-4 (2019)

Future developments. For the latest information about any future developments related to Form W-4, such as legislation enacted after it was published, go to www.irs.gov/FormW4.

Purpose. Complete Form W-4 so that your employer can withhold the correct federal income tax from your pay. Consider completing a new Form W-4 each year and when your personal or financial situation changes.

Exemption from withholding. You may claim exemption from withholding for 2019 if **both** of the following apply.

• For 2018 you had a right to a refund of **all** federal income tax withheld because you had **no** tax liability, **and**

• For 2019 you expect a refund of **all** federal income tax withheld because you expect to have **no** tax liability.

If you're exempt, complete **only** lines 1, 2, 3, 4, and 7 and sign the form to validate it. Your exemption for 2019 expires February 17, 2020. See Pub. 505, Tax Withholding and Estimated Tax, to learn more about whether you qualify for exemption from withholding.

General Instructions

If you aren't exempt, follow the rest of these instructions to determine the number of withholding allowances you should claim for withholding for 2019 and any additional amount of tax to have withheld. For regular wages, withholding must be based on allowances you claimed and may not be a flat amount or percentage of wages.

You can also use the calculator at www.irs.gov/W4App to determine your tax withholding more accurately. Consider using this calculator if you have a more complicated tax situation, such as if you have a working spouse, more than one job, or a large amount of nonwage income not subject to withholding outside of your job. After your Form W-4 takes effect, you can also use this calculator to see how the amount of tax you're having withheld compares to your projected total tax for 2019. If you use the calculator, you don't need to complete any of the worksheets for Form W-4.

Note that if you have too much tax withheld, you will receive a refund when you file your tax return. If you have too little tax withheld, you will owe tax when you file your tax return, and you might owe a penalty.

Filers with multiple jobs or working spouses. If you have more than one job at a time, or if you're married filing jointly and your spouse is also working, read all of the instructions including the instructions for the Two-Earners/Multiple Jobs Worksheet before beginning.

Nonwage income. If you have a large amount of nonwage income not subject to withholding, such as interest or dividends, consider making estimated tax payments using Form 1040-ES, Estimated Tax for Individuals. Otherwise, you might owe additional tax. Or, you can use the Deductions, Adjustments, and Additional Income Worksheet on page 3 or the calculator at www.irs.gov/W4App to make sure you have enough tax withheld from your paycheck. If you have pension or annuity income, see Pub. 505 or use the calculator at www.irs.gov/W4App to find out if you should adjust your withholding on Form W-4 or W-4P.

Nonresident alien. If you're a nonresident alien, see Notice 1392, Supplemental Form W-4 Instructions for Nonresident Aliens, before completing this form.

Specific Instructions

Personal Allowances Worksheet

Complete this worksheet on page 3 first to determine the number of withholding allowances to claim.

Line C. Head of household please note: Generally, you may claim head of household filing status on your tax return only if you're unmarried and pay more than 50% of the costs of keeping up a home for yourself and a qualifying individual. See Pub. 501 for more information about filing status.

Line E. Child tax credit. When you file your tax return, you may be eligible to claim a child tax credit for each of your eligible children. To qualify, the child must be under age 17 as of December 31, must be your dependent who lives with you for more than half the year, and must have a valid social security number. To learn more about this credit, see Pub. 972, Child Tax Credit. To reduce the tax withheld from your pay by taking this credit into account, follow the instructions on line E of the worksheet. On the worksheet you will be asked about your total income. For this purpose, total income includes all of your wages and other income, including income earned by a spouse if you are filing a joint return.

Line F. Credit for other dependents. When you file your tax return, you may be eligible to claim a credit for other dependents for whom a child tax credit can't be claimed, such as a qualifying child who doesn't meet the age or social security number requirement for the child tax credit, or a qualifying relative. To learn more about this credit, see Pub. 972. To reduce the tax withheld from your pay by taking this credit into account, follow the instructions on line F of the worksheet. On the worksheet, you will be asked about your total income. For this purpose, total

---

Separate here and give Form W-4 to your employer. Keep the worksheet(s) for your records.

W-4 — Employee's Withholding Allowance Certificate

Form W-4
Department of the Treasury
Internal Revenue Service

▶ Whether you're entitled to claim a certain number of allowances or exemption from withholding is subject to review by the IRS. Your employer may be required to send a copy of this form to the IRS.

OMB No. 1545-0074

2019

1 Your first name and middle initial Last name	2 Your social security number
Home address (number and street or rural route)	3 ☐ Single ☐ Married ☐ Married, but withhold at higher Single rate. **Note:** If married filing separately, check "Married, but withhold at higher Single rate."
City or town, state, and ZIP code	4 If your last name differs from that shown on your social security card, check here. You must call 800-772-1213 for a replacement card. ▶ ☐

5 Total number of allowances you're claiming (from the applicable worksheet on the following pages) . . . | **5** |
6 Additional amount, if any, you want withheld from each paycheck . . . . | **6** $ |
7 I claim exemption from withholding for 2019, and I certify that I meet **both** of the following conditions for exemption.
• Last year I had a right to a refund of **all** federal income tax withheld because I had **no** tax liability, **and**
• This year I expect a refund of **all** federal income tax withheld because I expect to have **no** tax liability.
If you meet both conditions, write "Exempt" here . . . . ▶ | **7** |

Under penalties of perjury, I declare that I have examined this certificate and, to the best of my knowledge and belief, it is true, correct, and complete.

Employee's signature
(This form is not valid unless you sign it.) ▶ _____ Date ▶ _____

8 Employer's name and address (**Employer:** Complete boxes 8 and 10 if sending to IRS and complete boxes 8, 9, and 10 if sending to State Directory of New Hires.)	9 First date of employment	10 Employer identification number (EIN)

For Privacy Act and Paperwork Reduction Act Notice, see page 4.   Cat. No. 10220Q   Form **W-4** (2019)

---

[14] "Public Document" W-4 Form, September 11, 2019

"This is a W-4. You will fill it out before you start a job and you can update it anytime. For example, if you have a kid or get married or divorced...whenever your life changes, you can fill out a new W-4."

I am still lost, along with everybody else.

Mr. Kyle takes notice. "Trust me, it isn't as hard as it looks. Before your first day of work, you will have to fill this out. Your first and last name...ah…your social security number, address, and..."

"I don't know my social security number!" Rebecca calls out.

"Me neither, omg."

Kyle puts his hands up. "Calm down, if you don't know it, ask your parents. Jot it down in a safe place or memorize it. You will *need it.*"

4 STEPS TO FILL OUT YOUR W-4

1.) See if you're exempt from withholding

2.) Fill out personal info & identify whether you're single or married

3.) Record total personal allowances

4.) Consider whether you want additional amount withheld

[15]

---

[15] Olya, Gabrielle. "The Complete Guide to Filling Out Your W-4 Form." GOBankingRates. Toggle navigation Back, March 21, 2019. https://www.gobankingrates.com/taxes/filing/how-to-fill-out-w4/.

I make a note to ask my parents about mine.

"So, the filling out part is easy, right? Boxes 1, 2, 3, and 4 are easy." We all agree.

"Now the tricky part is boxes 5, 6, and 7. These boxes are to determine your allowance and who you are claiming." Mr. Kyle pauses again.

I scratch my head.

"Remember this: once you begin earning money, you will have to pay income taxes. The purpose of this form is for your employer to know the right amount of federal income tax to withhold from your paycheck. When you get your paycheck, it seems like some of your money is missing, but it's due to the taxes coming out. This is the difference between gross and net income."

Gross income - what you make before taxes

Net income - what you make after income tax is taken out (paychecks are net incomes, not gross)

"So, they take money out of your paycheck to pay Donald Trump?" Max asks.

"Not exactly," Mr. Kyle answers. "I know it sucks, but it is necessary. The taxes from everyone's paychecks go to goods and services provided by the Federal Government, even if not everyone agrees with it. You aren't responsible for taking the taxes out, your employer is."

Taxes pay for [16]

- Social Security, Medicare and Medicaid
- Public education
- Military
- Roads and highways
- City planning, etc.
- Correctional facilities
- Science programs
- Farming/Goods
- International affairs

"So, does everyone understand why employers take money out of your check?"

We nod, and Mr. Kyle continues, "For box 5, you have to determine who you are claiming as a dependent."

Dependent: someone who you provide over fifty percent of their support (money) to, for example a child or a relative through blood or guardianship.

*Dependents can't make over a certain dollar amount (gross income) *

"Since you guys are in high school and your parents probably still support you, you would be unable to claim yourself so you would claim zero."

"Here are some examples. Just remember, the more allowances you claim, the fewer taxes will be taken out of your paycheck."

---

[16] Huddleston, Cameron. "This Is Where Your Tax Dollars Actually Go." GOBankingRates. Toggle navigation Back, February 21, 2019. https://www.gobankingrates.com/taxes/filing/where-do-tax-dollars-go/#2.

<u>Examples of what people can claim on their taxes:</u>

- a spouse
- children
- themselves
- Note: if parents claim you, you aren't allowed to claim any allowances on your W-4

"Okay, box 6 is asking, do you want to withhold money from your check? Simple, right?"

"So, should we put a number down on this box? I had my mom fill this out for me, she put down zero," Maria comments.

Kyle gives Maria a thumbs up, "Yes, zero is fine. No need to give the IRS extra money out of your paycheck." Mr. Kyle takes a deep breath, he continues, "Alright, the last box is number 7. It means you don't owe the government anything. So, if you don't owe the government any money, you can write exempt."

Things to remember:

- April 15th is the last day to file your taxes.
- You can get an extension upon request
- If you don't file taxes you may owe penalties, back taxes, and interest.

"A W-4 is required by law, and anyone who gets wages has to file a return. If you paid too much taxes throughout the year, you will get a refund check. If you don't pay enough, you will owe. Ideally, you want the same amount that was taken out during the year to equal the amount you owe in taxes[17]."

---

[17] Dwight, Bill. "Teach Teens What a W-4 Is For." Family Finance Favs, January 1, 1970. http://www.familyfinancefavs.com/2016/04/teach-teens-what-w-4-is-for.html.

Chapter 8: *The Startup*

Mr. Kyle sighs. Ms. Brown hands him a bottle of water. He takes a big gulp. "Does anyone have any last-minute questions?"

"Yes, I have a question," asks someone sitting at the back of the room.

"Okay, shoot." Kyle takes another gulp of water.

"Both my parents are business owners and…I'm thinking I want to start one too. Am I too young to have my own business? And if not, how do I go about doing that?"

I look over my shoulder and recognize the guy from around school.

"What is your name?' Kyle asks him.

"Blake."

"Okay Blake, you are not too young to open a business. In fact, opening up a business is not as hard as it looks. You just need a plan, do the research, and to learn the rules." Kyle smiles.

"So..." Blake chuckles.

"So, a business starts with a passion, a need, or a great idea. What is your passion?"

"Uhh-"

"Your passion could be anything, sports, animals, maybe writing," Kyle interrupts him. "Before you start a business, find your passion or come up with an idea."

"I'm passionate about film. I think I want to become a screenwriter."

64

"Nice, that can be turned into a business. Now you need to write a plan, but before you do all that, you must follow these steps."

Steps to Starting a Business.

1. What is your passion or your talent?
2. Do you have any skills?
3. Can either your skills or talent generate money?
4. What resources would you need?
5. Will your business provide a service or sell a good?
6. Who is your target market? Or demographics?

Hmmm, I have this incredible dope business idea! This is what I'm talking about. Finally, we are learning about how to start a business. I know exactly what I'm going to do. I'm going to design my own skateboards from old boards and sell them for mad cheap! I could fix them up kind of like how people fix up old cars. I already have a name and everything:

Sean's Skate and Design.

Sounds pretty legit, right? I have been thinking about this for quite some time. I'm pretty good at sketching, too. I think my target market would be like teens and cool adults. Yeah, I know some pretty cool skaters that are adults. I'm pretty good at fixing boards, too. I feel like I got the first six steps covered.

"If you guys are stuck on what type of business you can start, here are some ideas for kids your age."

Top 10 Teen Business Ideas

- Baby/Pet/House Sitting

- Social Media Influencer

- Car Washing Service

- Graphic & Web Designer

- Clothing Designer

- Photographer

- Podcaster or Blogger

- Tutor

- Lawn Care

- Errand Service

[18]

---

[18] Pilon, Annie. "50 Business Ideas for Teens." Small Business Trends, June 19, 2019. https://smallbiztrends.com/2016/10/business-ideas-for-teens.html.

"Let's say starting a business isn't really your thing. Some of you guys might be too busy. You can definitely have a side hustle. And some of you might need a side hustle or part-time job to help start your business."

"Okay, next up let's talk about how to legitimize your business. Maria, what is the name of your business?"

"Huh...well, I'm going to have a business called Lit Nails...it is going to be fantastic."

"Lit nails...okay, who is your target market?"

"Um, women like in their twenties and thirties."

"What kind of women?"

"You know, women who are super girly like me and high maintenance. See, I get my nails done every two weeks." Maria shows her hot pink nails to everybody.

"Okay, okay, how many workers are you going to hire and how much profit do you think you will make?"

"Dang, Mr. Kyle I haven't thought about all that."

Mr. Kyle laughs, "No worries, that is what a business plan is for. After you come up with a business idea, you need to write up a business plan. You need to figure out how much money you will need for your business, if you will be using your own money or whether you need a loan from a bank or will need investors. It all depends how big or small your business will be. You have to figure out if you are going into business for yourself or if you think you will be hiring people."

Limited Liability Company "LLC"

Pros:

-Limited liability for owner

-Can be taxed as sole proprietorships, partnerships, or corporations

-Can add members

-Easier fundraising

Cons:

-Need to register with the state and pay registration or filing fees *amounts differ by state

-Subject to state laws governing LLCs

[19]

---

[19] "LLC vs. Sole Proprietorship." legalzoom.com, September 10, 2018.
https://www.legalzoom.com/articles/llc-vs-sole-proprietorship.

Sole Proprietorship

Pros:

-Ease of setup

-Generally less costly than LLCs

-Don't have to keep annual corporation records

-You are management

Cons:

-100% responsible for all business debts and obligations

-Typically more difficult to raise operating cash

-Appears less professional

[20]

---

[20] O'Connell, Brian. "Sole Proprietorship vs. LLC: How Do They Compare in 2019?" TheStreet, January 2, 2019. https://www.thestreet.com/personal-finance/education/sole-proprietorship-vs-llc-14821236.

"When you are just starting out, you get a chance to pick what route you want to take. Whether your business is an LLC or Sole Proprietorship[21] is up to you. You can also consult with an attorney or tax attorney to help determine what structure is right for you and your business. If you are doing something like food catering, I would get an LLC. Food is very hard to manage, for example customers could potentially get sick and blame this on your company. If you have an LLC, it would protect you from being solely responsible. If you are selling t-shirts or something like that, sole proprietor might be a better option for you."

"Mr. Kyle, how much money do you think we will need for our businesses?" I asked him.

"Some may need a lot and others might not need as much. You have to remember that a business is an investment. You aren't going to get rich with a snap of a finger."

Mr. Kyle picked up on my disappointment.

"If you were to research your favorite company, you would be surprised about their humble beginnings."

I nod my head.

"Okay guys, we are running out of time." Ms. Brown looks at her watch. "Any last-minute questions, before we close out?"

"I do have one last question...."

Everyone looks at me, I don't really know how to ask this question, but this is something that has been on my mind....

---

[21] "Why You Should Form an LLC vs. Sole Proprietorship." Incfile. Accessed September 12, 2019. https://www.incfile.com/blog/post/form-llc-vs-sole-proprietorship/.

"Like…," I begin, "I'm confused. I have adults in my ear every day talking about how I need to go to college. I need to learn math and all this other stuff. I feel like…I don't need it to get where I want to be," My hands begin to shake. "My parents are doctors and I don't want to be that. I want to be something else…you know."

Mr. Kyle frowns. He then gives me this serious look.

"I'm not going to stand here and say that everyone should go to college and I also won't say you don't need college. The truth is that college is worth it, but it may not be the route you need to take to be what you want to be."

"That makes sense," I answer.

Mr. Kyle smiles, "I didn't go to college, but I had a plan. If I didn't have a plan, I would have been out here selling my mixtapes or something."

Brandon hollers. "Bruh, I'm weak."

"But it is the truth, there are so many people in the workforce that aren't working in their field. To them, theirs is worthless," Mr. Kyle says.

"And also, there are people who don't go to college and or trade school who are stuck in dead-end jobs," Ms. Brown adds.

"Well, that isn't going to be me." I shake my head no. "I got a plan."

"It doesn't have to be you. College is a stepping stone to success, but it isn't the only step you can take. We all can't follow the same path because we are all not the same. Find what you want to do, make a plan, and stick to it as best you can."

Hailey
The Model

Chapter 9: *Plan, Plan, Plan*

My name is Hailey McIntosh. I am a junior at Lakewood High. School is okay as far as I can tell. I am super busy. I don't have time to go to the football or basketball games or really do anything: I model. Everyone thinks I am famous. I have like 10,000 followers on IG and Teen Vogue follows me. It's kind of a big deal - I walked in my first fashion show last Fall. It was so dope. Most people here have dreams of becoming a pediatrician or a lawyer, but my dream is to go big.

I want to go to Paris and become bigger than Kendall Jenner. I have the ambition to make it, I can see myself gracing the cover of Italian Vogue, eating pastries in Milan, and walking down runways across Europe.

I take modeling seriously. You can say I was born for this. Everyone thinks so and I'm starting to think I am, too. When I am not in school, I am taking classes, doing catalog shoots, and shopping. God, I love to shop so much so my mom took away my credit card. So, I am here at *The Money Club* to learn how to "finance" or something like that. Well...actually, my mom said if I attend one session then I can get my credit card back. So today, I canceled my shoot to go to this Money Club thing. I need to learn how to budget before I move to Europe and live on my own. Budgeting should be easy. I have heard around school that *The Money Club* was cool. I don't know Ms. Brown, but they say she is nice.

I get to the classroom. I look around, trying to find a familiar face, I spot Jason sitting near the back with a group of people; everyone knows him. Superstar athlete: tall, broad shoulders, built legs, he could model, too. I sit in the front. I put my iPhone on silent and pull out my notebook. More students pour into the classroom.

"What's up, everyone?"

I look up and I notice Mrs. Jones, smiling hard next to another woman with a bun on her head. Oh, that is Ms. Brown. She smiles. I check out her clothes. She looks like she has some style. I like her already.

"Today, we are going to talk about something that everyone needs and that is budgeting."

A few people groan. Mrs. Jones and Ms. Brown chuckle.

"Does anyone know why budgeting is so important?" she asks as the PowerPoint comes on.

"It helps you save money," someone calls from the back.

"Yes, it can."

"It is like a plan for your money," a freshman girl with glasses next to me says.

"If you ain't got no money, take your broke hmmph on!"

The class hollers. I turn my head around to see who said that. It was the stocky kid next to Jason. Even Mrs. Jones and Ms. Brown are dead. See, this is why I love Mrs. Jones; she is so chill. I took PreCalc with her last semester, I got like a high B and I suck at math: Mrs. Jones is that *good*.

"Annie is right, budgeting is a plan for your money. It can help you save money and it can help you reach your money goals. It also tracks spending."

"Do we have to budget though?"

"Yes, everyone should budget, even rich people."

"Yeah, 'cause they rich."

"Look." Mrs. Jones gets real stern. "If you can't manage and budget one-hundred dollars then you will not be able to manage one-

76

thousand dollars. If you stick to your budget, I have no doubt you will reach your financial goals." Mrs. Jones shrugs. "Seems easy right?"

I nod my head. I see what she is saying. A few people say yeah.

"So how do you budget?"

"Good question, in order to budget you first have to track how much you spend."

"And how do we do that?"

"You check your bank account activity, you keep your receipts, or you write out everything you buy...."

"No offense but who has time for that?"

"Do you have time for IG and Snapchat?"

"Got 'em!"

"Hold up, to make this concept easier I want you guys to think of checking and tracking your spending the same way you think of checking your IG or FB feed. Call it the money feed. The money feed will show you your spending habits, whether good or bad." Mrs. Jones raises an eyebrow.

Yikes, I think she is talking about me. I definitely need to track my spending, because I have a few bad habits I need to axe asap.

"So, by checking your money feed you can check how much money comes in and how much money comes out; that is your cash flow."

I think I got it. Cash in and Cash out. Tracking spending. It doesn't sound like biology. I repeat it a few more times until my brain clicks. I noticed a few other people focusing on their thoughts too. It makes me feel better. I'm not the only one thinking this hard.

"When tracking spending, you should include every single thing you use your money for, whether it is bills, gas, food, personal items, and *shopping*," Mrs. Jones continues.

"To write an effective budget, I would start by writing it out for two weeks. Usually, people will say write out a monthly budget. But you guys are young and most of you will get paid every two weeks. This will make things easier. But first let's look at your previous spending, going back about a month or so."

"How would you do that?" I ask.

"Do you have a bank account?"

"Yeah…but it is linked with my mom's."

"Ask your mom, if you can look at your account activity. You can look online or download your bank's app. There, you can find your banking account activity. It will tell you how much you use your debit card. If you do not have a bank account, I would advise everyone to get one. But for today, I want everyone to list out what you spent your money on last weekend, whether it is a want, need, or bill! Take five minutes."

I open my notebook up. I know I used my credit card a lot and I use my debit card a lot, too. I sigh and begin to jot down everything I can think of:

<u>Weekend spending</u>

Friday:

>Salad from Chopt $13.50
>Bottle water $2.00
>Yoga Class $20.99

Saturday:

>Gas from Exxon Mobile $20.00
>Smoothie from Smoothie King $8.95
>Reese's from Target $1.25
>Movie with Becca and Adrianna $10.95
>Popcorn and bottle water $7.25
>Summer Cardigan from Boutique $19.99
>Bracelet and Scarf $8.50
>Thai peanut butter zoodles $15.99

Sunday:

>Brunch from Zack's Dinner $12.99
>Sun Glasses from Body wave $42.63
>Pizza from Dominos $10.00

"Now that you have done that, I want you guys to add up how much you spent this weekend. Some of you all be prepared to be shocked." Mrs. Jones chuckles.

I take out my phone and punch in the numbers. Thirteen dollars and fifty cents plus two dollars plus…twenty dollars and ninety-nine cents is…thirty-six dollars and forty-nine cents…not too bad. . .I calculate the rest and I get a total of one hundred and ninety-four dollars and ninety-nine cents. Wait. $194.99! Omg that sounds like a lot. I look back at what I spent, there is absolutely no way I spent that much money in like two days. I hear other people with the same sentiments.

"So...guys...how much did you spend?"

"Man, Mrs. Jones...This is crazy. I spent a lot of money this weekend," someone yells from the back.

I turn my head around again. The stocky kid looks stressed. So does the girl next to Jason who...well...he looks like *Jason*.

"How many people spent more money than they thought they had?"

Over half of us raise our hands. I instantly feel better.

"Well, you check your Instagram feed every day, right?"

I chuckle.

"You should check your money feed too. How many of you didn't spend that much money?"

A few raised their hands.

"Let's say you spend that much money every weekend for a month. I want you guys to multiply your total by four."

I multiply my total and I let out a loud groan. $779.96! I'm in complete shock.

"We aren't done yet!!!!! Now multiply that number by twelve."

I quickly do what she says. The number blows me away: $9,359.52.

"It adds up, doesn't it?"

My mind is completely blown! I let out a low groan. This might be why I don't have access to my credit card anymore. I swear I will never use it again. I mean the price of living in Paris is scary and if I can't get a grip now...

"Keep in mind, that wasn't even your daily spending. I bet you guys don't pay many bills or take care of any needs. I bet everything you spent was all wants. Am I right?"

I check over my weekend list. To be honest, the only thing I truly needed was gas on Friday. I shake my head. I don't shop as much as I used to but...I still eat out too much.

"Mrs. Jones, what about food?" someone else asks.

"You got to remember, groceries are food, groceries are a need. Eating out is a want! You can save money by cooking at home or eating leftovers!"

The class groans again. I shake my head again. I hate leftovers...that reminds me, I will probably be eating leftover pizza for dinner...great. Chewy bread and yesterday's cheese. Hmm, I could stock up on protein bars. But those are expensive too. Ugh...

"I know this is frustrating," Mrs. Jones says.

It's like she is reading my mind!

"You need this reality check. You can spend a lot eating out especially when you are eating three times a day! Even if it is 4 for 4 at Wendy's."

That 4 for 4 is good though, but I could hold off maybe for a month.

$ $ $ $ $ $

"Now, I know most of you guys have jobs." Mrs. Jones laughs, "But, before you get that first paycheck you might need to get hip to that budget and check your money feed."

Ms. Brown cracks up. They are loving this!

"When I was young and dumb, I didn't spend my first paycheck wisely." Ms. Brown and her glance at each other smiling while shaking their heads.

Neither did I, apparently.

"For those of us who don't have jobs yet, what should we do with our very first check?" The girl beside me asks.

"Well, for your first paycheck follow this advice:"

BE SMART WITH YOUR
FIRST CHECK

-Don't go shopping and blow your money all in one day

-Write a list of all the things you want in order of greatest want to least want

-Write out all the things you NEED

-When shopping, don't fall for impulse buys

-Pay off any bills you may have

"When you get your first paycheck, it is going to feel good, better than an allowance! For those who have an allowance, we will talk about that in a second. Real quick, what are some things you guys are dying to buy?"

"I want to buy a new skateboard."

"A couple of books."

"The new 2k."

"Jordans!"

Mrs. Jones shrugs her shoulders. "That sounds good and all, but what about something big? What are you guys saving for? Don't answer now, this is a rhetorical question."

I think about everything I want in life and the things I really want. I know I need tons of money to move to Europe, I think I heard someone say $10,000. I have nowhere near that amount of money saved up.

"Relax y'all, a budget will save the day. Take a Woosah."

Everyone takes a deep breath.

"A budget is something that everyone can master, ease your mind."

"This is a budget guide," Mrs. Jones says, making air quotes. "Your budget may look different, but as long as it is similar to this one, it will be easy-peasy." Mrs. Jones grins.

"I'll print out some example guides in case anyone needs one," Ms. Brown tells us.

Income	Budget	Actual
Job #1	$	$
Job #2	$	$
Allowance	$	$
Other income	$	$
Total	**$**	**$**

Expenses	Budget	Actual
Fixed		
Rent	$	$
Car Insurance & Payment	$	$
Student loan	$	$
Credit card debt	$	$
Phone	$	$
Varaible		
Travel (Gas, Parking, Tolls)	$	$
Food	$	$
Entertainment	$	$
Clothing	$	$
Miscellaneous/Other	$	$
Total	**$**	**$**

"Mrs. Jones?" I ask. "Can you explain fixed and variable expenses?"

"Yep, fixed expenses do not change. They are a fixed amount like a phone bill or car insurance. On the other hand, a variable expense changes, like how much you spend on groceries or doctor visits."

Fixed Expenses and Variable Expenses:

(f) fixed: unchanged expenses: car insurance, phone bill, Netflix, Spotify

(v) variable: food, gas, groceries, clothes

"So how do you keep track of your money feed if your variable expenses change?" she asks.

"Maybe, cut back on some of them?" I answer.

"Precisely! Some months you are going to have situations where you spend more on your variable expenses and you will have to adjust your budget. If you want to save money for that big thing, you have to adjust your spending! Remember, don't break it, adjust it." Mrs. Jones clears her throat. "I have some scenarios in the next few slides to help you grasp this concept better. Take a look."

SCENARIO 1: COURTNEY

- Courtney is a high school junior who lives at home with her parents
- She gets a $50 allowance every week from her parents and sometimes babysits on the weekends
- She doesn't have a car yet but tries to put $250 a month aside for a car

"First Scenario, Courtney earns $200 a month from her allowance and for babysitting she earns $180.00. All together she earns $380.00 a month. Courtney is saving for a car for college. If her income doesn't increase for the next two years, she would need to save $250 a month for a $6,000 used car."

Courtney's Money Feed:

Week 1: Monday- $10.00 for Chipotle
        Tuesday- $1.50 School Lunch
        Wednesday- $1.50 School Lunch
        Thursday- $2.00 Fries, $3.00 Hamburger School Lunch Deluxe,
        $9.99 Netflix
        Friday- $1.50 School lunch, $5.00 Starbucks, $7.00 Lakewood JV
        Football

Week 2: Monday- $1.50 School Lunch
        Wednesday- $4.00 Pan pizza School Lunch Deluxe
        Tuesday- $9.25 Chick-Fil-A
        Thursday- $1.50 School Lunch, $3.50 Snacks at gas station.
        Friday- $2.00 Fries School Lunch Deluxe, $1.50 Regular lunch
        Saturday- $12.00 Stationery from Barnes and Noble.

Week 3: Monday- $1.50 School Lunch
        Tuesday- $2.50 School Lunch with drink
        Wednesday- 1.50 School Lunch
        Thursday- $5.00 Hamlet School play
        Friday- $1.50 School Lunch
        Sunday- $5.00 Starbucks

Week 4: Monday- $2.00 Fries, $3.75 Chicken Tenders School Lunch
        Deluxe
        Tuesday- $1.50 School Lunch
        Wednesday- $8.25 Smoothie from Juice Breeze
        Thursday- $1.50 School lunch
        Friday- $1.50 School Lunch, $7.00 Varsity football game
        Saturday- $7.00
        Sunday- $6.99 Mascara, $4.00 Lip gloss

Income	Budget	Actual
Job #1 (Babysitting)	$150	$180
Allowance from parents	$200	$200
Other income	$0	$0
Total	**$350**	**$380**

Expenses	Budget	Actual
Fixed		
Rent	$0	$0
Savings for a Car	$250	$250
Student loan	$0	$0
Credit card debt	$0	$0
Phone	$0	$0
Varaible		
Travel (Gas, Parking, Tolls)	$0	$0
Food	$50	$80
Entertainment	$50	$50
Clothing	$0	$0
Miscellaneous/Other	$0	$0
Total	**$350**	**$380**

"Courtney did pretty good, however, do you notice anything she could've done better?"

"Uhhh...well maybe she can cut back on food, like make her food at home or something," Rebecca calls out.

"Right, right, anything else?"

"Maybe she needs to be more aggressive with her savings, too, and she can find other things to do with her friends besides going to the movies," I say.

"Exactly. When you have a financial goal, like saving up for a car, you do need to be more aggressive with your savings." Mrs. Jones smiles. "Here is a tip: extra money needs to pay off high-interest debt first or to beef up your savings! It is tempting to spend extra money for wants rather than needs."

I feel like Mrs. Jones is talking to me. I so need to stop eating at Chipotle every day, but it is so freaking good.

"Okay, next one."

My attention snaps from Chipotle to the PowerPoint.

SCENARIO 2: JESSIE

~ Jessie is a high school senior who lives at home with his parents
~ He works 25 hours a week at a clothing store in the mall
~ He drives his dad's old car that's paid for but he's in charge of gas & other car expenses
~ Any extra money at the end of the month goes towards savings for college

"This is Jesse, he is a senior and works part-time at a sporting goods store. He has multiple variable expenses and he is trying to save for college. Keep in mind, Jessie is making $7.25 an hour. Weekly he is making $181.25 and $725 a month. Let's check Jessie's money feed."

Jessie's Money Feed:

Week 1: Monday- $50.00 Car Insurance, $1.50 School Lunch
Tuesday- $300 Savings College, $1.50 School Lunch
Wednesday- $1.50 School Lunch, $3.00 Toll road
Thursday- $35.00 Gas, $1.50 School Lunch, $3.00 Toll Road
Friday- $1.50 School lunch, $22.00 Joggers, $3.00 Toll Road
Saturday- $5.00 McDonalds
Sunday- $4.00 Wendy's, $12.00 Movies

Week 2: Monday- $5.00 McDonald's breakfast, $1.50 School lunch
Tuesday- $8.00 Burger King, $3.00 Toll Road
Wednesday $1.50 School lunch, $30.00 Groceries and snacks
Thursday- $1.50 School lunch, $3.00 Toll Road
Friday- $1.50 Lunch $65.000 Oil change
Saturday- $6.25 Waffle house $3.00 Toll Road
Sunday- $9.00 uber, $18.00 Video games

Week 3- Monday- $5.00 gas $10.00 Parking ticket $1.50 School lunch
Tuesday- $12.00 Socks, $1.50 School lunch, $3.00 Toll Road
Wednesday- $5.25 McDonald's, $1.50 School lunch, $1.50 Toll
Thursday- Phone $85.00, $1.50 School lunch, $1.50 Toll Road
Saturday- $10.00 gas, $1.50 School lunch, $12.00 Movie, $3.00
Friday- $1.50 School lunch
Sunday- $6.01 Uber

Week 4- Monday- $5.00 gas $1.50 School Lunch, $3.00 Toll Road
Tuesday- $1.50 School lunch, $10.00 parking ticket $3.00
Wednesday- $1.50 School lunch $8.00 Dave and Busters
Thursday- $22.00 Windshield wipers, $3.00
Friday- $33.99, Toll Road
Saturday- $8 Uber
Sunday- $0

Income	Budget	Actual
Job #1	$800	$950
Job #2	$0	$0
Other income	$0	$0
Total	**$800**	**$950**

Expenses	Budget	Actual
Fixed		
Rent	$0	$0
Car Insurance	$50	$50
Student Loan	$0	$0
Credit card debt	$0	$0
Phone	$85	$85
Saving for College	$100	$300
Variable		
Travel (Gas, Parking, Tolls)	$260	$250
Food	$150	$100
Entertainment	$75	$50
Clothing	$80	$50
Miscellaneous/Other	$0	$0
Total	**$690**	**$885**

"What is one thing you see looking at Jesse's money feed?" Mrs. Jones asks.

"He saves for college as soon as he gets paid…" Brandon speaks up.

"Yeah… that is pretty smart. He actually saved more. Let me take notes." says Max.

"Look at you guys catching on fast! Jesse did a great job with keeping track of his money feed, which means he matched or spent less than the amount of money he budgeted for. He has $65 left over, and with that amount, he can save for an emergency fund[22]."

"Is an emergency fund something everyone needs?" I ask. I know my mom has always told me to put extra money aside in case something happens. But lately, I haven't been saving any money.

"Yeah, emergency funds are used in case you are stuck in a jam. For adults, emergency funds are a must. It is good to have at least three to nine months of expenses worth of savings set aside. Financial setbacks can be catastrophic."

"Wait," I fly my hand up.

"Yes," Mrs. Jones answers me.

"It's cool that Jessie was able to save early, but he still spent more than he should."

Mrs. Jones tilts her head. A huge smile spreads across her face, "Technically, you are right…*but* not everyone saves for the same things." Mrs. Jones heads to the whiteboard.

---

[22]An emergency fund is a large amount of money set aside in case something financially catastrophic happens.

Primary Savings
- Emergency cash fund
- Car
- College
- Prom
- Graduation rings
- Savings account
- Food

Secondary Savings
- Designers sneakers: Nike, Air Jordans, Adidas, Puma
- New phone
- Concerts
- Senior trips

"You all have different things you will want and need to save for. If I were you, I would prioritize your savings goals and break it down to these two categories."

"Noted…." I give Mrs. Jones a thumbs up.

"Now, that we got that *saved* away. Any other questions before we get to the final scenario?"

"So… even young people like us, need an emergency fund?" Rebecca asks.

"Precisely, life happens even to your average 'teenager'. Like for example, car accidents and speeding tickets."

I groan. I remember my first speeding ticket. Lakewood cops do not play!

"Or what about, if you leave all your money in your sock drawer like Mrs. Lawrence told you not to and somebody steals it!" Ms. Brown shouts while coming into the class with papers.

"I got you, Ms. Brown, I'm opening up an account tomorrow," Brandon calls out.

Ms. Brown gives him a thumbs up and begins to pass out the budgeting guides.

We erupt with laughter.

$ $ $ $ $ $

"Okay, last scenario. We are almost done!

SCENARIO 3:
HOLLY

- Holly is a college freshman living in a one-bedroom apartment
- She works 35 hours a week at a coffee shop
- She has a car but unfortunately received a speeding ticket this month

This is Holly. Holly is a college student who works full-time. She is great with managing her money, however, her recent speeding ticket has her in a bind. Yikes."

As Mrs. Jones is speaking, I wince thinking about that speeding ticket.

"You might be thinking Holly makes a lot of money, she doesn't need to budget. But budgeting benefits everyone including millionaires. Listen, you got to live inside your means. You can't have a caviar taste on a peanut-butter-and-jelly budget."

That is so me, but what can I say, I love nice things.

"We all love nice things; but try not to spend too much," Mrs. Jones says.

What in the world! Swear, this woman is a psychic.

"Let's check out Holly's money feed."

Holly's Money Feed:

Week 1: Monday- $900 Rent, $200 Car insurance
Tuesday- Utilities $46.00
Wednesday- $15.00 Dice salad bar
Thursday- $0
Friday- $3.99 Starbucks
Saturday- $6.00 Parking
Sunday- $0

Week 2: Monday- $100 Groceries Target Supercenter
Tuesday- $20.00 Gas
Wednesday- $12.00 Panera Bread
Thursday- $4.15 Dunkin Donuts
Friday- $25.35 Black leggings Old Navy 2 for 2
Saturday- $15.00 Walmart
Sunday- $0

Week 3- Monday- $5.50 Parking
Tuesday- Spotify $9.99
Wednesday- Parking ticket $350.00
Thursday- $20.00 Eyebrow and armpit waxing
Friday- $88.00 Court fees
Saturday- $25.00 Trader Joe's Groceries
Sunday- $8.00 Cafe

Week 4- Monday- $8.25 YouTube premium
Tuesday- $15.00 Gas
Wednesday- $8.12 Starbucks
Thursday- $33.00 Monthly Student parking
Friday- $17.00 Movies
Saturday- $75.00 Phone bill
Sunday- $0

Income	Budget	Actual
Job #1	$1,500	$1,500
Job #2	$0	$0
Other income	$0	$0
Total	$1,500	$1,500

Expenses	Budget	Actual
Fixed		
Rent	$900	$900
Car Insurance & Payment	$200	$200
Student loan	$0	$0
Credit card debt	$50	$0
Phone	$75	$75
Insurance	$0	$0
Variable		
Travel (Gas, Parking, Tolls)	$100	$150
Food	$135	$100
Entertainment	$40	$40
Clothing	$0	$0
Miscellaneous/Other	$0	$500
Total	$1,500	$1,965

"Did anyone notice that Holly spent a lot of money compared to the others?"

A few of us nod.

"Mo' money, mo' problems!"

"Ain't that the truth," Ms. Brown says.

"What happens as you make more money, you tend to buy more stuff. You want to upgrade your lifestyle, but upgrading your lifestyle causes more expenses. As you can see with Holly's money feed, she spends more due to rent, car insurance, etc. but that's life."

I take out my phone and set a reminder to write a budget this week. I am Holly, literally.

"Now, what sticks out to you about Holly's budget?"

"She spends the most on rent," I say.

"Yep, what can she do to remedy that?"

"Find a roommate, my brother has one," Max says.

"How about move back home? Or find a student apartment?" Mrs. Jones adds.

The class nods.

"She can also save money on gas by walking or taking a bus, because her parking tickets rack up." I chime in.

"Yes, yes she can. Anybody else?"

"Maybe find restaurants that take student discounts," Rebecca says.

"Also, she could shop for different car insurance, to see if she can get better pricing."

"Get rid of some of her subscriptions…?"

"Now you all are getting it!" Mrs. Jones sits on the desk. She smiles at us. "If you are overspending, check your money feed and cut out unnecessary expenses to get your budget back on track!"

"Cash in and Cash out," we all say.

Mrs. Jones claps in excitement. "So, who will write a budget for the upcoming week?"

Sean, Rebecca, me, and a few other students raise their hands.

The Money Club ends, people begin to leave the classroom. I stay behind trying to take in all the information I heard today. I look over everything and add a couple of notes to what I have. Someone taps me on the shoulder. I look up. It is Mrs. Jones beaming down at me.

"Hailey, how are you? I didn't think you had time for activities outside of school."

I laugh, "Yeah, you are right. But I kind of put some stuff on pause since I found out about this club. And I'm glad I came."

Mrs. Jones nods, "I'm glad you came, and don't get too stressed about all this information. It isn't Calculus."

I smile, she is right. I take a deep sigh. I wave goodbye to both her and Ms. Brown. I might go to some more classes. This was so beneficial. I need to make it a priority. But it is going to be hard trying to juggle *The Money Club* in Spring. It is about to be bridal season and I will be booked. I shake my head; I can't think about that right now. I don't want my brain to melt.

I walk out the front doors at Lakewood. A few of the people in the club are hanging out waiting for their parents to pick them up. I spot Jason and nod at him. He gives me a thumbs up along with the stocky kid. He is such a dork! The girl next to him waves at me. I smile and get into my car. A feeling of accomplishment comes over me. I literally feel empowered; I can't wait to show my mom my budget. She is going to be so proud and I'll have my credit card back in no time!

Responsible me, adulting me, my eyes widen. You know what, I'm not going to eat out for a whole month! That will definitely save me money. I need to write a list out of all my goals, my money feed, my budget, my spending and everything. I race home trying to beat five o'clock traffic.

Chapter 11: *Everything Will Fall into Place*

The bell rings for lunch. I dash to the faculty break room to heat up my lasagna. Brownie points for me. This is the first time in a long time, I brought my own lunch. After the last club meeting, I realized my spending habits could use a little tweaking.

When I got home, I printed out my bank and credit card statements, cancelled my magazine subscriptions, and revisited my budget for the previous months: rent and my car note take out chunks of my paycheck, not to mention, I am paying off two student loans, and two credit card payments: frivolous spending.

My morning trip to Starbucks and my online shopping is eating away at my extra cash. I don't even need to go to Starbucks; my parents gifted me a Keurig months ago. Eating out is another dagger in my budget, but I like the convenience. It is so easy to go to Starbucks before work and shop online.

I considered canceling my Netflix account, but Netflix originals are too good. I decided to take a break from going out and bring food to work. I finish heating my lunch and as I head out the door, I smack straight into Mr. Davis. His papers fly in the air.

"Mr. Davis, I am sorry. I didn't see you there."

Mr. Davis swoops down to pick up the fallen papers. I crouch to assist him.

"No worries, Ms. Brown, I didn't see you either."

The papers from his manila folders are scattered across the floor; lucky for us the hallway isn't too busy. Mr. Davis' papers are a mixture of quizzes, homework, and classwork: the deadly three. I decide to sort them out as I grab each of them to make it easier on him. He follows suit, putting the papers in the piles as I sort them.

"I wasn't good at Trig," I say, cutting the awkward silence.

"Not too many people are," Mr. Davis replies as he finishes packing the folders. "So, how are things going with your Cash Club?" he asks.

"You mean *The Money Club*..." I hand him the last folder. He takes a moment to check his watch.

"Yes, yes, *The Money Club*, are things well?" Mr. Davis half-smiles.

"Things are going well. Last week there were thirty students in attendance," I grin, anticipating his reaction.

"Oh, really?" Mr. Davis' eyebrows raise.

"Yes," I clear my throat, preparing to shock him with more good news. "You remember Elijah? The predicted valedictorian." I wipe some hair out my face, preparing to lay the good news on thick.

"Yes, he is in my first period."

"Well, his dad wants *The Money Club* to expand...maybe even be a course offered next year." I stand up and Mr. Davis follows me, clearing his throat like he is choking on something.

"Wow, I never expected..."

I turn around, "Why don't you come to the next meeting, Mr. Davis?"

He looks at me and looks down at his watch again. "Uhh, maybe, I don't know, one of these days."

"Do what you can," my grin widens. A feeling of satisfaction runs through my entire body. I wish I could say, "I told you so" or something to rub it in, but I don't. I refrain, he catches my drift.

Since *The Money Club* has been rolling, I can tell it's making a difference. Brandon has even completed a portion of his study guide. Actually, I think all my students have done a good portion of their study guides. Mr. Davis and I say our goodbyes and I strut to my classroom.

When I get there, I eat my lunch and write out my plans for my next two classes. I save the last ten minutes of lunch preparing slides for today's club meeting. I can't wait for school to let out. I am pretty excited for today's subject. My dad, a financial expert, is coming in to talk about something we all struggle with: investing. Investing can be a big scary word. I'm looking forward to today's club meeting for sure.

Ashley
The Quiet Genius

Chapter 12: *Think On The Dime*

The teachers at school tell me college is worth it, but my family doesn't think so. I don't know who to listen to. On one hand, I need a job to help out at home, "college doesn't pay the bills" my dad says. On the other hand, my school counselor says education is the key to success and I want to be successful.

Neither of my parents went to college. I do have a cousin who went and dropped out. I hope to be the first in my family to go and graduate. I want to be an electrical engineer. They make tons of money. My parents don't have enough money to send me to college; they think I need to get a job. I heard you can get a scholarship to pay for school, I am determined to get one.

I stop and look over what I have written. English class isn't my strong point, but I have gotten better at writing. I am a nerd, but only when it comes to numbers. Every day in English, we journal the daily prompt at the end of class. Today the prompt was:

Is college worth it?

I think it is. Being the oldest of five, I have to set an example for my younger brothers and sisters; I'm not allowed to make any mistakes. If I go to college, they will want to go, too.

"Everyone, we have a quiz on *The Great Gatsby* tomorrow!" Mrs. Figueroa yells after us as the bell rings.

I am the last one to leave. I take it slow to avoid the crowded hallways and drag my feet to Ms. Brown's class. After third period, everyone is sluggish. I know I am. The afternoon crash always gets to me. During weeknights, I am studying and babysitting my siblings or kids from the neighborhood. It's like I take care of everyone.

I grab a granola bar from my backpack. I always carry one with me for an afternoon pick me up. I get to Ms. Brown's class just in time, before the late bell. In Algebra II, I don't speak to anyone - I'm a freshman - well, the lone freshman. The "cool" kids sit in the middle chatting and laughing, and the rest of us sit in the front or wherever is left. I go to class, do my work, and leave. I duck my head as I pass by Ms. Brown's desk. I plop down in the chair next to the window.

Everyone is on their phone or talking. Me, I don't have a phone. Mom says I can't get one until I turn sixteen, which means we can't afford it. I grab my math book and binder out of my bookbag and work on the bell assignment. I can hear some of the kids talking about *The Money Club*, the one Ms. Brown created for teaching personal finance.

The next meeting is this afternoon, hopefully I'll be able to make it. I missed the first couple of club meetings - I had to help my mom with the twins. I made the last one, though.

Ms. Brown starts the timer for the bell ringer. I fly through the math problems, less than ten minutes.

"You got extra paper?" Sean taps me on the shoulder.

I take out a stack of paper from my binder and hand it to him.

"Thanks for looking out."

I politely smile. Sean always asks me for paper. He is the only one who speaks to me. It used to be annoying, but it is something. Class goes like this: Ms. Brown says something, Brandon and Jason protest or the entire class groans, Ms. Brown goes over something new and no one pays attention.

Towards the end of class, Ms. Brown collects our homework. I hand her mine.

"Ashley, are you coming to *The Money Club* today?"

"Ummm… I think so."

"Well, definitely come. My father is coming, he will be talking about investing."

"Wait, Ms. Brown, did you say your pops?" Brandon yells out.

"Investing?" I say out loud.

"Yes, Ashley, investing. I need a brain like you in there." Ms. Brown turns to me and winks.

My cheeks burn; I didn't realize I said that out loud.

"I'll see how it is, Ms. Brown."

Brandon and a few of his friends laugh. Ms. Brown heads back to the front of the class and the bell rings. After class, I head to the front office to use the phone: I'm going to call my mom and tell her I can't babysit tonight. I have to go to the club today, we are talking about investing!

$ $ $ $ $ $

I get there early. Ms. Brown and her dad are up front. He is dressed in a black suit. I sit a few seats up from my usual seat. Students pour into Ms. Brown's room. A few of them I know, like Brandon, Jason, Rebecca and Sean, but there are also other students I haven't seen before. Every seat is filled.

"Hey guys, I'm Ms. Brown's dad, Nathaniel," he says.

"You can call me Mr. Brown. I have been a financial advisor for professional athletes for ten years." Mr. Brown grins. "Before we begin, I have a question for you guys."

The PowerPoint lights up the room.

WHAT WOULD YOU
CHOOSE??

$1,000,000
Today

A penny doubled
every day for 30
days

23

"If I gave you the option to receive one million dollars right now or a penny doubled every day for thirty days, which would you choose?"

Hands go flying up and Mr. Brown laughs. "Wow, I can tell you guys are eager."

"You, what is your name young man?"

"Uh...Brandon."

"Okay, Brandon. Which would you choose?"

Brandon smirks, "Mr. Brown, you have to hit us with something harder than that. I'm taking the mil."

Jason and a few other kids burst into laughter.

23 "Compound Interest." Vimeo, September 12, 2019. https://vimeo.com/288577833.

"Bruh, I am taking the $1,000,000 too," someone else shouts out. Brandon and Jason give each other a high five.

Mr. Brown cackles, "Okay, okay! Anybody else want to answer?"

I know the answer. It is simple. If the penny is doubling every day for thirty days, it will be way more than $1,000,000. It's like exponents. Simple math. I glance around the room. Mr. Brown is still waiting for an answer. I raise my hand a bit.

Ms. Brown sees me. A soft smile spreads across her face, "Ashley, would you like to answer?" she asks.

The whole class turn their attention to me. My heart flutters.

Mr. Brown points at me. "What would you choose?"

Chapter 13: *The Great Equation*

"I'd take the penny doubled every day for thirty days."

As soon as I say it, chaos ripples through the room, like I said the unthinkable.

"What the..." Brandon jerks his head back at me. "You would take the penny over a million dollars?!"

My cheeks burn. Mr. Brown interrupts him by holding up a big hand to say, "Hang on. Why don't we work through the math," Mr. Brown quickly writes on the board.

> Day 1: .01
> Day 2: .02
> Day 3: .04
> Day 4: .08
> Day 5: .16
> Day 6: .32
> Day 7: .64
> Day 8: 1.28
> Day 9: 2.56
> Day 10: 5.12

"After ten days, the penny doubling is about $5." Mr. Brown looks around the room. "The milli is looking real nice huh?"

Brandon stands up and throws his hands in the air. "See, the million is the better choice!"

Sean nods his head in agreement.

"Let's keep going! By day twenty, our penny isn't doing so bad!"

Day 11: 10.24
Day 12: 20.48
Day 13: 40.96
Day 14: 81.92
Day 15: 163.84
Day 16: 327.68
Day 17: 655.36
Day 18: 1,310.72
Day 19: 2,621.44
Day 20: 5,242.88

"Our penny is over $5,000 now and we still have 10 more days!" Mr. Brown scans the room.

"Is anyone thinking about changing their minds now?"

Day 21: 10,485.76
Day 22: 20,971.52
Day 23: 41,943.04
Day 24: 83,886.08
Day 25: 167,772.16
Day 26: 335,544.32
Day 27: 671,088.64
Day 28: 1,242,177.28
Day 29: 2,684,354.56
Day 30: 5,368,709.12
Day 31: 10,737,418.24

Mr. Brown flips to the next screen.

WHAT WOULD YOU
CHOOSE??

$1,000,000

2^30
1,073,741,824 cents
= $10,737,418.24

23

"This is wild," Hailey says, Max agreeing with her from across the room.

Mr. Brown laughs again. "This is an example of compounding interest. Think of compounding interest as interest on steroids. Compounding interest is a powerful way to make your money grow faster." I think he is enjoying wigging us out.

"That is a lot of money!" Brandon yells.

"Yeah, it is." Mr. Brown and Ms. Brown laugh.

"So…how many of you guys are making money?" he asks us.

A few of us raise our hands. I sort of make money, well, technically, if you count babysitting.

"Good, good. Who can tell me what they do to make money?"

"I'm a lifeguard!"

"I work at the mall, in the food court!"

"You got me on a discount, right?!" Mr. Brown smiles.

We all laugh.

"Okay, that sounds great! How many of you guys save the money you make?"

Fewer people raise their hand this time.

"I'm saving to buy a car!"

"I spend my money on makeup and food," Rebecca chimes in.

"College," a couple of people shout in unison.

"Okay, we have some smart savers in here! What about investing? How many of you invest?"

No one says anything.

"Okay, well like I said before, I work with professional athletes!" As Mr. Brown is talking, he places three bottles on the desk.

Mr. Brown tells Ms. Brown to pass out fake money to the room.

"Here, I have water, an electrolyte drink, and a soda. If you guys were professional athletes, which one will add the most value to your body on game day? Come up and place your money where your mouth is." Mr. Brown grins again.

Everyone rushes to the front. I wait until most people are walking back before I get up. I can't decide between water and the electrolyte drink. A lot of people put their money on the electrolyte drink; I mull over the two and I finally place my money in front of the water bottle—you need water to live. I walk back to my desk and sit back down, hoping I made the right decision. Mr. Brown inspects the baskets of money.

"Well…from the looks of it, not a lot of you put your money with the soda, can someone tell me why?"

"Soda is bad for you. I would never put that in my body. I need my body to be right on game day," Jason calls out, "But after the season…I'm drinking it, Mr. Brown."

"Good point! But, not everyone agrees; can anyone tell me why they choose soda?"

"It's got caffeine. Sometimes before practice, I drink it for the extra energy boost," Brandon says.

"Yeah, that was probably one of those practices you got a cramp in huh?" Jason teases and Brandon makes a face.

We all laugh.

"Moving on, the water and electrolyte option looks like they have the same amount of money, who wants to explain?"

"Well…I'd drink both, like I drink water all day, but when I'm working out, I need the electrolyte to restore what I lost. So, I put my money for the drink," says Hailey.

"Can anyone tell me why they picked water?"

I lock eyes with Ms. Brown, maybe I should say something…I raise my hand again. I am more confident than the last time.

"Yes?"

"Um…I picked it because everyone needs water…"

"Got it. Let's say, you did play in the basketball game, those who put their money on soda, caught a cramp during the game lost money."

"Awe man," a few kids say.

"Those who put their money in water, got water belly, didn't perform as well as they usually do, but scored the winning basketball. Your money doubled."

"I'd take that, though," Max replies.

Well at least my money doubled, that makes me feel a lot better.

"Those who put their money in electrolyte drink, got a triple double, and their money tripled."

"What did I tell you." Jason reaches his hand out to Brandon who smacks it away playfully.

"I like the enthusiasm. Based on this example, guess what you guys did?" Mr. Brown waits for us to answer. He clears his throat, "You guys showed me you have a basic understanding of how investing works. That is good stuff. Many of you already invest, maybe not with money, but with time and energy towards studying for an exam, playing a new sport, or learning a new language."

"Like my trainers for basketball?'

"That's right! You invest in your trainers to perfect your craft to earn a basketball scholarship." Mr. Brown adjusts his tie and rocks from one foot to the other.

"Well…I invest in my technique and skills on my skateboard. If I want to be a pro, I have to invest the time," Sean explains.

"See? What did I tell you? You are already investing time in things you love to do. And you guys are getting a return. For you, the return is 'I will go pro'." Mr. Brown turns his direction to Sean, "Let's say you have a big test coming up, you spend your time investing by studying for the test. If you study, you will more than likely get the grade you want. Get it?" Mr. Brown asks us, his voice rising with expectation.

"When you think of investing money, that is when things can be confusing. But trust me, it is simple. I know many of you use money to buy items like video games or new sneakers. But unlike time, studying equals a good grade. Investing your money in shoes won't get you anything back. In other words, those items don't come with a return." Mr. Brown walks to the other side of the room.

"Think of it like this: investing is putting your money into a company or a project where you will get a return. If you invest your money, your return will be money back."

"Let's see...let's say you start your own YouTube channel, because your friend did and started making money from it. You buy a laptop and a camera, and you work on your material, in hopes to make money off your channel. This is an example of investing in items in the hopes of making money from your investments."

I nod my head.

"So, investing does come with some risk. Let's say you post fifty videos and you don't get the engagement you were hoping for, because you don't have many subscribers or likes, companies aren't sending you free stuff, and you aren't getting paid for your content. Now you feel like, buying the camera was a waste of money because it didn't pay off."

"Ohhhhh, I get it, I bought all this stuff hoping to make a profit?" Sean asks.

"Yes."

"But I need to get the stuff to start my channel though."

"And that is where the risk comes in. No risk, no reward," Mr. Brown grins.

That totally makes sense, I like where this is going.

"So, investing makes your money grow," Max asks.

Mr. Brown nods his head, "It can. Let's dive into it."

Mr. Brown chuckles again as he notices our confused faces. "The good thing is there is no right way to invest, but the one thing most analysts can agree on is you have to be diversified."

Hailey raises her hand, "What do you mean?"

"Take a look."

Types of Investments

- **Stocks**

- **Bonds**

- **Mutual Funds**

- **Real Estate**

- **Savings/Certificates**

of Deposit

- **Collectibles**

[24]

---

[24] "Types of Investments." Adults. Accessed September 14, 2019.
https://handsonbanking.org/adults/planning-future/investing-basics/types-of-investments/.

"This slide shows different types of investments. Investing in a few of these listed, is what I mean about diversified." Mr. Brown clears his throat. "You never just want to invest in one thing, you want to keep your portfolio diverse. Don't just invest in stocks, but invest in stocks, mutual funds, bonds, etc."

We nod in agreement as Mr. Brown continues.

"What I want you guys to remember is, each investment carries some type of risk, some more than others. The greater the risk, the higher the return."

"Um, Mr. Brown, what do you think is the riskiest investment?" I ask.

"Awe...on average, stocks."

"What are stocks?"

I shift in my seat and lean forward, maybe stocks is a way I can earn extra money or something.

"When you think of stocks, I want you guys to think of ownership. When you own stock, you own a small percentage of the company you choose to invest in."

"How do I know what to invest in?"

"Great question. My advice is to invest in what you love! Let's do an exercise. Take out a piece of paper and a pen or pencil." Mr. Brown clasps his hands together. "I want you all to think about a typical Saturday. Play it out in your head and write down companies and brands you use or see. Follow my lead," Mr. Brown says.

"Last Saturday, I checked my *Rolex* and realized it was time to go. I put on my *Nike* sweatsuit and *Jordans* and got my *Spalding* out of the garage. My son and I got in my *Corvette* and stopped at *BP* on the way to basketball practice. Now, you all try."

I begin to write down my Saturday, but I don't have a lot of brand name stuff. Unless you count Eggo, I eat that almost every morning. I do put on my Sketchers and go bike riding, but I can't remember what brand my bike is.

"Yo, Mr. Brown, so I could like, own Apple?" Jason looks up from his paper with big eyes.

"You sure can, you can also own what you wear."

I look down at my Old Navy jeans.

"I see you guys are catching on. Now I want you guys to write down a list of your favorite companies."

Companies I use:

Internet: Google, Intel
TV: Discovery, Netflix
Fashion: Old Navy, Huggies, Vans
Money: MasterCard, BB&T
Food: Wendy's, Tyson, Nature's Own

I think I have everything I use. Ohhh, Lysol. That is another one I add.

"Are you guys done writing down your list?"

"Yes," we reply.

"Good, so if you guys choose to invest in these companies, they can help you make money. When they make money, you make money. But if they lose money, you lose money."

"Wow... is it worth it to invest?" Rebecca asks.

"Yes, history shows, owning stock is one of the best ways to increase wealth."

"But I'm not trying to lose money......"

Mr. Brown chuckles. "No one wants to lose money! It will also be beneficial to research the company you will be investing in. Corporations have to put out Corporate Reports and Financial statements, so you can see how they are doing. You can find this on the company websites."

Rebecca groans.

"Before you dip your toes in the stocks, we need to go over stock indexes."

"Okay, what are those?" Rebecca asks.

"Have you ever heard people say the stock is 'up' or 'down'?"

"Yeah."

"Well, a stock index tells you how a group of stocks is doing. It will tell you how your company is doing on the market. Can you imagine looking at individual stocks? There are too many stocks to count! A stock index will save you time, and if you look at them, you will have better success in investing[25]." Mr. Brown cuts a look at Rebecca.

"How many stock indexes are there? I am interested too," Sean says.

"There are tons, but for young people and teens - beginners if you will, you need to know three."

"Wait, why do you need to know three?" asks Rebecca.

---

[25] Boneparth, Douglas A., and Heather Boneparth. The Millennial Money Fix: What You Need to Know about Budgeting, Debt, and Finding Financial Freedom. Wayne, NJ: Career Press, 2017.

"They are the most commonly used," Mr. Brown responds.

BASIC STOCK
MARKET INDICATORS

Dow Jones Industrial Average (DOW)

-30 leading industrial stocks

-single most watched

Standard and Poor's 500 Index

-500 of the largest U.S. publicly traded companies

-more accurate than DOW

-evaluates a greater variety of stock

National Association of Security Dealers Automated Quotations (NASDAQ)

-monitors technology companies

-speculative stocks, show dramatic up and downs

[26]

[26] Merritt, Cam. "What Are the Differences Between the Dow Jones, NASDAQ & S&P 500?" Finance, March 5, 2019. https://finance.zacks.com/differences-between-dow-jones-nasdaq-sp-500-5513.html.

"As you can see, the Dow, NASDAQ, and Standards and Poor's 500 are the most common stock index. They are very helpful in determining what stocks to invest in. Keep in mind, there are more than the three listed!"

Everyone nods. I write some notes down. I have been wanting to learn this stuff since last summer, spending a lot of time at the library. When I first read about this stuff, I was so lost, but now it is making some sense.

"Well, how do we make money by investing in stocks?"

"You make money, with Stock Dividends & DRIPs." Mr. Brown looks at me and smiles.

"Dividends will provide a steady income. Companies will give out dividends quarterly. Usually, dividends are paid in cash. If you really believe that the company will do well, you use that cash to buy more shares in the company, and that is what DRIP is." Mr. Brown pauses, "The next way to earn money with investing in stocks is buying and selling stock. When you buy stocks, it is best to buy more than one share, then you can sell them when the stock rises to make a profit, or you can hold on to them.

"Well, how do I like...start?" I ask.

"Yeah, I would like to know, too," says Rebecca, backing me up.

"You just start."

We all groan.

Mr. Brown glances at his watch, "Ahh...unfortunately, we have run out of time."

Aww man.

"But I am so glad you guys are excited about investing. You guys can buy and sell investments at any time. If you want to know more, I would advise you check with an advisor at your bank," Mr. Brown says, "or, you can check with a financial planner and financial publications such as newspapers, websites, and T|V."

Mr. Brown closes out. I go over my notes, making sure I have added everything I need to know about investing. I can go to the library this weekend to check out a book. I know I am pretty young, but I have seen videos on YouTube about teens investing. If people younger than me can do this, then so can I.

Jason
The NBA Bound Star

Chapter 15: *Plan B*

Beads of sweat drip down Dre's face as he is telling his story. Mrs. Jackson, our guidance counselor, hands him a towel. He takes a swig of water, wipes his forehead and then takes a deep breath
.

"It was the biggest game of the season," Dre lowers his voice.

"We were playing Franklin County in the 2nd round of state playoffs. Friday night games at my high school are like the Super Bowl. I am the top linebacker coming out of North Carolina, named defensive breakout player of the year, and tonight, I planned on putting on a show for my hometown; I bleed Cougar blue and white."

"It was the beginning of the third quarter and I'd been on the quarterback's ass all night, already recorded two sacks. Not to mention the three TFL's and five solo tackles. It's third and long and my team needs me to make a stop. If the offense gets the first, they'll have a chance to tie the game. I can't let that happen."

"'Blue 32, Blue 32, Set, Hut!' Franklin's quarterback yells. It's showtime."

Dre is a big guy; he is way taller than me, and I am 6'2. He has to be at least 6'5, and big. I didn't know Ms. Brown knew any big-time athletes. Ms. Brown said he was a motivational speaker now. I checked him out. He has 50k followers on IG and 1 million views on YouTube. We have had many people come in a speak, but a retired NFL player? Crazy man. Anyone who made it to the league gets mad respect. Period.

"The quarterback faked the handoff to the running back, then pitched the ball to the tight end. There's a hole in the o-line, and he is coming right for me. No way I am letting him get this first down. I see red. I need to take this guy out! I take off: Wrapping my arms around his body, I slam him. Bam! My teammate Tae gets double teamed and overtaken, crashes to the ground. My legs get caught under him and I can't get up."

Dre looks at me.

"Do you know what it's like to be pinned to the ground by a 6'3", 309-pound defensive lineman?"

I shake my head. I've never even touched a football. Dre stares at his hands like he has never seen them before and takes a deep breath.

"I remember, I was on the ground, numb and shocked. The whole world had stopped. I hear somebody shouting my name: 'Dre! Dre! Dre!' In my mind, I answered, 'I'm here, I'm okay,' but I can't talk. It was all coming back to me, what happened - the crowd, the music, the band...everybody was waiting on me. I'm like, man, how did this happen?"

Dre frowns.

"I'm in pain. My knee hurts, the adrenaline from the game is wearing off, and the discomfort sets in as I realize I tore my ACL. Coach Ward is holding my hand and tears are running down my face. All I can think is, 'Damn, my career is over.'"

I swallow, that's tough. I've seen ACL injuries in real life; but hearing him talk about it makes me feel weird.

"What if your dreams don't pan out? Do any of y'all have a plan B?"

I don't need a plan B. I have been playing basketball my entire life. I have been on the best travel teams since I could dribble. I know what it takes to be a college athlete. I'm going to go pro.

"I heard you were a baller?" Dre points at Brandon.

I look at Brandon.

"Nah, I'm talking to you," Dre cuts his eyes at me.

"Uh, I play a bit," I try to sound cool. I smile at Rebecca. She rolls her eyes at me.

"Okay, okay, you nice?"

I laugh. I am the number one shooting guard in the state.

"I'm okay," I answer. I don't want to sound too cocky; I mean, this guy played in the league.

"Do you have good grades."

I shrug my shoulders.

"Have you ever been hurt before?"

"No," I shrug again. Everybody is looking at me, including Mrs. Jackson and Ms. Brown. "I'm in shape and I eat pretty good."

"Do you have any official offers?"

"Yeah, I have a few."

"What happens if you get seriously injured?"

I shrug my shoulders again. I haven't thought about. I mean, I highly doubt I will get hurt, and if I do, I'll bounce back. I look at Dre's knees; he has a scar on each of them. His quads are huge, it is hard for me to imagine him hurt. My teammate Jonathan tore his ACL in the beginning of the season. But Jonathan is big; he is carrying extra weight. I know NFL and NBA players tear things and stuff, but they are back real quick, like my man Russell Westbrook. He's had two knee surgeries and is still explosive.

"I'll rehab like Russell Westbrook," I say.

Brandon gives me a pound.

"Okay, I got you, but you aren't in the NBA yet, you might not have access to the best trainers and doctors...you wanna know something, what's your name?"

"Jason," I answer.

"Jason, before that game, the top schools in the nation were gunning for me: Alabama, Clemson, LSU, Oregon, and NC State. After the game, those schools were nowhere to be found."

"Were you able to bounce back?" I say calmly.

"I played at the college level and I tore my ACL again. I put all my money into football and when I got hurt, it was over. I didn't have a Plan B."

I nod. But one thing about me is I don't plan on having a Plan B. If I don't make it to the league after my freshman year, I plan on trying again when I am a sophomore. Too easy. Dre looks directly at me.

"Now, if I didn't have good grades coming out of high school, I would have never made it into any school that was looking at me. You might be talented, but if you don't have the grades, you won't make it. You are a student-athlete. Schoolwork comes *first*."

Chapter 16: *College Bound*

Mrs. Jackson stands up. "School *does* come first. Everyone, give Dre a hand."

We all clap as Dre sits down.

"Hello everyone, I am excited to be here today, I have heard great things about *The Money Club*." Mrs. Jackson smiles extra wide. "I brought Dre in today because I want you guys to understand how important life is after college, whether you want to be an athlete, or a scientist, or even a homemaker. I want you guys to really think about your future."

Mrs. Jackson writes on the board:

What do you want to be when you grow up?

Annie raises her hand, "What if you don't know?"

"Good question, if you don't know I would advise you guys to come see me or go to your guidance counselor and take a career assessment. If you don't know what you want to be, ask yourself what you want to do and what are your interests."

"Ok, I used to want to be a tennis player, but it is hard getting a scholarship," Max says.

"Awe, that is the next thing I was going to talk about."

"I know some of you play sports and want to continue to play in college, but I want you guys to pay attention to the participant numbers of both High School and NCAA."

Estimated Probability of Competing in College Athletics

	High School Participants	NCAA Participants	Overall % HS to NCAA	% HS to NCAA Division I	% HS to NCAA Division II	% HS to NCAA Division III
MEN						
Baseball	491,790	34,980	7.10%	2.10%	2.20%	2.80%
Basketball	550,305	18,712	3.40%	1.00%	1.00%	1.40%
Cross Country	266,271	14,350	5.40%	1.80%	1.40%	2.20%
Football	1,057,382	73,063	6.90%	2.70%	1.80%	2.40%
Golf	141,466	8,527	6.00%	2.10%	1.70%	2.20%
Ice Hockey	35,210	4,199	11.90%	4.80%	0.60%	6.50%
Lacrosse	111,842	13,899	12.40%	2.90%	2.30%	7.10%
Soccer	450,234	24,986	5.50%	1.30%	1.50%	2.70%
Swimming	138,364	9,691	7.00%	2.70%	1.10%	3.10%
Tennis	158,171	7,957	5.00%	1.60%	1.10%	2.30%
Track & Field	600,136	28,595	4.80%	1.80%	1.20%	1.70%
Volleyball	57,209	2,007	3.50%	0.70%	0.70%	2.00%
Water Polo	21,286	1,013	4.80%	2.70%	0.70%	1.30%
Wrestling	244,804	7,175	2.90%	1.00%	0.80%	1.10%
WOMEN						
Basketball	430,368	16,532	3.80%	1.20%	1.10%	1.50%
Cross Country	226,039	15,966	7.10%	2.60%	1.80%	2.70%
Field Hockey	60,549	6,066	10.00%	3.00%	1.30%	5.70%
Golf	75,605	5,372	7.10%	2.90%	2.10%	2.20%
Ice Hockey	9,599	2,355	24.50%	8.80%	1.20%	14.50%
Lacrosse	93,473	11,752	12.60%	3.70%	2.70%	6.20%
Soccer	388,339	27,638	7.10%	2.40%	1.90%	2.80%
Softball	367,405	19,999	5.40%	1.70%	1.60%	2.10%
Swimming	170,797	12,684	7.40%	3.30%	1.20%	2.90%
Tennis	187,519	8,736	4.70%	1.50%	1.10%	2.10%
Track & Field	494,477	29,907	6.00%	2.70%	1.50%	1.80%
Volleyball	444,779	17,387	3.90%	1.20%	1.10%	1.60%
Water Polo	20,826	1,159	5.60%	3.40%	0.90%	1.30%

[27]

"Wow," I hear a kid in the front whisper.

"Wow is right," Mrs. Jackson replies.

---

[27] Smeyers@ncaa.org. "Estimated Probability of Competing in College Athletics." NCAA.org - The Official Site of the NCAA, April 9, 2019. http://www.ncaa.org/about/resources/research/estimated-probability-competing-college-athletics.

"This table shows how many high schoolers go on to participate in sports at the college level, but it also shows there are more athletes who participate in college sports than there are scholarships available for that sport," explains Mrs. Jackson.

Mrs. Jackson looks at me, "Not every athlete in college has a full-ride scholarship. Full scholarships are determined by the sport of play, the division of the sport, and the money available. Some sports don't offer full scholarships. They may offer partial scholarships, this is why you need to have good grades and why you need a Plan B."

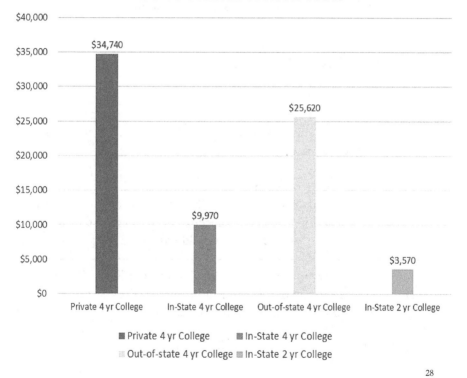

AVERAGE COLLEGE TUITION COSTS

28

---

28 Goldy-Brown, Sarah. "The Average Cost of College in 2018 - Student Debt Relief." Student Debt Relief | Student Loan Forgiveness. Student Debt Relief |

"This was the average cost of college in 2018. Higher Education is one of the biggest investments you can make. The cost of tuition is growing at an exponential rate. Student loan debt is a serious issue for college grads. Please note, other expenses such as room and board, books and supplies, transportation etc., aren't included in the graph."

I listen to Mrs. Jackson talk, zoning in and out.

"Judging by this graph, how much you pay for college depends on the type of institution and your residential status," Mrs. Jackson smiles again, "To save money, maybe consider going to a community college first, or consider schools in your state. Notice the difference in tuition on the graph in 4 and 2-year schools and in-state versus out-of-state."

"I'm thinking about going to community college or to a trade school," Brandon says.

"Yes, trade school is a good option as well. You can go to trade school to obtain your certifications for the job market. Those certifications will separate you from the rest of the pack."

Brandon and other people nod their heads. I nod my head along with everybody else. I stare at the slide. Private school is mad expensive. I know my grades are decent enough, but I don't think I could make it at a private school...I would have to really pay attention.

I look at Brandon; his eyes are glued to the PowerPoint. Dre's story is still fresh in my mind. I'm not gonna lie, I'm a little anxious. I have gotten mad interest from multiple schools, but you know it is all about the fit. I'm supposed to be verbally committing in a few weeks...I think about signing day as Mrs. Jackson's lips are moving.

Student Loan Forgiveness, May 9, 2019.
https://www.studentdebtrelief.us/news/average-cost-of-college-2018/.

LOANS	SCHOLARSHIPS	GRANTS	WORK STUDY
-Direct Subsidized	-Athletic, Academic,	-Federal Pell	-Need Based
-Unsubsidized	Leadership,	Grants	-10-15 hours
-Perkins	Theatre,	-FSEOG	a week
-PLUS	Music	-State	-Paid directly
-Private Loans	-Competitive	Grants	to student
	-Institutional	-Institutional	-Generally
	-National, State, Local, or Civic	Grants	above min. wage

"Okay, in this slide we have ways to pay for school: loans, scholarships, grants, and work-study. Dre talked about scholarships for Student Athletes. It is important to remember at some schools you cannot receive a full athletic scholarship. You would have to find additional ways to pay for school."

Mrs. Jackson glances at me.

"Not everyone will be a student athlete, but there is good news, there are other scholarships out there."

"Like...academic scholarships?" Ashley says.

"Yes, there are many scholarships out there you can apply for, academic among others. You can also apply for grant money at the state and federal level, if your parents cannot afford college."

"How do we go about finding scholarships?" Ashley asks again.

---

[29] For more resources on how long it will take to pay off a student loan check out the free resources at the back of the book.

"I can see someone is thinking," Mrs. Jackson smiles. "You can find this information out when you apply for FAFSA, anybody know what FAFSA is?" Mrs. Jackson calls on Max.

"Isn't it like something to help you get money for college?" Max asks.

"Bingo! FAFSA stands for Free Application for Federal Student Aid. Instead of talking you guys to death, I can show you what it looks like. Take a couple of minutes while I pull up the site."

Mrs. Jackson walks over to the laptop.

---

[30] "FAFSA®: Apply for Aid." Federal Student Aid, September 26, 2019. https://studentaid.ed.gov/sa/fafsa.

"Two things you need to know about FAFSA is one, it is required if you want to qualify for any kind of federal financial aid, and two, October 1st is the first day you can apply. I will write the steps on the board."

Steps to sign up for FAFSA:

1. Make a login. As of May 2015, the FSA ID consists of a user-created username and password.

2. Select the year you're applying for (Reminder: The FAFSA must be filled out each year and Oct 1st is the first day it can be completed).

3. Fill out all Personal Identification Information.

4. Then create your profile by adding school info, parent info, and financial information. You may need a parent for this step!

"Make sure you've taken good notes and be ready come October 1st to apply! I understand some of you may have already heard about the FAFSA, but you may not know all the FACTS. These are what you need to know."

FAFSA
Facts v/s Myths

MYTH: My parents make too much money

FACT: There is NO income cut-off to apply

MYTH: I don't want to borrow money with loans

FACT: The FAFSA doesn't just give loans they also determine if you qualify for grants at the federal and state level

MYTH: There's no rush to fill out my FAFSA

FACT: On average, students who file within the first 3 months tend to receive double the grants

[31]

---

[31] Helhoski, Anna, Anna Helhoski, Anna, Teddy Nykiel, Associated Press, NerdWallet, and Associated Press. "Top 10 Financial Aid Myths Debunked." NerdWallet, March 22, 2019.
https://www.nerdwallet.com/blog/loans/student-loans/top-10-fafsa-myths-debunked/.

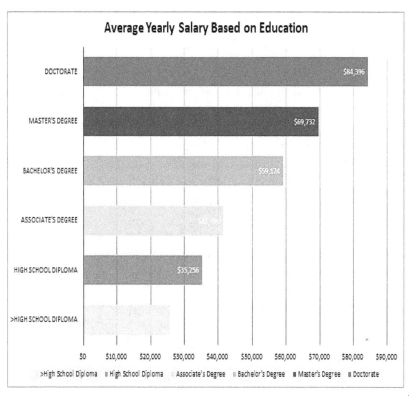

Average Yearly Salary Based on Education

32

"We have talked about how expensive college is, but not attending college can hurt your career and in turn hurt your financial future. Finally, I want to talk to you guys about how college can determine your future." Mrs. Jackson takes a sip of water, "Back in my day, you could get a good job straight out of high school. Now, there

---

[32] Josephson, Amelia. "The Average Salary by Education Level." SmartAsset, May 15, 2018. https://smartasset.com/retirement/the-average-salary-by-education-level.

are increasing educational requirements for jobs. Times are constantly changing."

"Mrs. Jackson?" Max asks.

"Yes...?"

"What if I don't want to go to college or don't have a knack for higher learning?"

"I would like to add something on this." Dre stands up. "There are more educational avenues you can take. You don't have to take the traditional route. You can go to trade school, take night classes. A buddy of mine joined the Airforce at eighteen and now he is studying to be a pilot."

"Ahh, yes," Ms. Jackson beams, "The military, is there anyone interested in joining the military?"

Rebecca raises her hand.

"What, you want to be a soldier?" I ask her.

Rebecca shrugs, "I mean you don't have to be a soldier to be in the military, right?"

"Rebecca is right, you don't have to be a soldier, there are many jobs you can do in the military, the same jobs that are out here, are available in the military and in some cases cooler jobs like pilot and coast guard."

"Also, the military has education benefits as well as benefits for life," Dre adds.

"Cool, who can we talk to?"

"Next week, we have a recruiter coming Tuesday and Thursday, also at Lakewood we do have ROTC. If you are interested, come by my office and sign up." Ms. Jackson flashes another smile, "Dre, do you have anything else to add?"

"Ahh...I think we covered everything." Dre grins.

$ $ $ $ $ $

The club lets out.

I hug Rebecca before she leaves and walk out with Brandon to take him home. Before I get into the car, I see a clean Mercedes pull up. The windows roll down. It's Dre!

"What's up?" He flashes a smile.

"This your whip?" Brandon asks.

"Yep, she is mine."

"Nice," I say.

"Yeah, it is nice. Listen, I know you kids are ready to go to the league and whatnot, but I wanted to give you guys my business card."

Dre reaches into his pocket and takes out two cards from his wallet. One for me and one for Brandon. On the front of the card, it's a photo of Dre and on the back in a football uniform.

"I didn't get to mention this in the club meeting, but after I got hurt in the NFL, I knew I wasn't going to have a second chance again. So, I decided to use another talent of mine, my voice. I have spoken to a lot of people across the country telling my story and letting kids know they have options. Shoot, I even got a book coming out soon."

"Dang, for real," Brandon says.

"Yeah, you may not have listened to everything I said, but hear me out. There are bigger things out there than ball. Even if you don't make it to the league, you can still make an impact. It's always a good thing to have options and a Plan B."

"FACTS," Brandon gives Dre a fist pump. I look down at my sneaks.

"Aye, you listened today."

I shrug my shoulders, "A little bit," I replied.

Dre strokes his beard.

"I know, you young, you don't think about the future, kids live in the present, but don't forget what I said. Alright?"

"I got you," Dre reaches out his hand and I grab it.

"Talent will only take you so far, you have to use your head."

I give Dre a nod. I hear him.

Rebecca
The Preppy Chick

Chapter 18: *I will pay you back*

I don't go to a bad school, but it is definitely nothing like my last one. I've been here at Lakewood for a semester. I transferred from Brier Academy, a private school. My dad got a new job, we packed up, moved across the state, and now I am here. At my old school, the classes were small, and the books were new. When I came to Lakewood, I traded my boring uniform for something more chic. And I don't mind it here. I am passing all my classes, making new friends, life is good.

The bad thing about switching schools is I have to take Algebra II again. Lakewood is definitely behind in academics. The sports here are crazy good though! The boys' and girls' basketball teams are reigning state champions, and the football team made a deep run in the playoffs. Sure beats Brier Academy. I don't think I ever witnessed a winning season for any sport, unless you count Robotics Club.

I didn't think I was going to make any friends here, but there is this one kid I'm crushing on, Jason, a future NBA superstar. You could say we are "talking". My first day at Lakewood he sat right next to me in math class and asked me to his game.

Before the Money Club, he made a fuss about his coach making him go. He asked me to tag along and I did. So far, the Money Club is cool. We have been talking about topics I have learned from my parents; I have a checking and savings account. And my dad gave me a credit card I can use in emergency situations. But I am learning new stuff and relearning things I forgot about. When we worked on budgeting with Mrs. Jones, I realized I spend too much money on shopping. I have enough clothes! Since then, I haven't been to the mall once and I am saving a ton!

$ $ $ $ $ $

"This is the last day of *The Money Club!*" Brandon announces as we walk through the trailers.

"We made it!" he shouts. Jason and Brandon give hive fives.

I roll my eyes. These guys, they act like this all the time. Brandon and Jason crack up. I laugh too - I can't help it. We stop at the stairwell. Brandon sits on the rail and Jason and I sit on the first step.

"Jason? What did you learn in *The Money Club*?"

"Uhhh...I learned I need a Plan B."

"Brandon, what did you learn?" I put my hand on my hip.

"I mean, I learned a lot."

"Nah, what did you learn fool," Jason laughs.

Brandon rubs his chin.

"I learned not to claim none of y'all asses on my taxes!"

"Brooooo, shut up!" Jason slaps Brandon's neck.

I shake my head, "Forget it, guys." I check my phone. "Y'all, let's go, we don't want to be late for the Money Club."

"Okay, *Ms. Brown*," Jason teases.

$ $ $ $ $ $

When we walk into the class, music is blaring. Did she forget we were having The Money Club or something?

[Interlude]

"You wanna know what's more important than throwin' away money at a strip club? (Credit.) You ever wonder why Jewish people own all the property in America? This how they did it."

A hard beat is in the background like hip-hop, old school...what in the world is Ms. Brown listening to?

[Verse 2]

"I bought some artwork for one million

Two years later, that sh*t worth two million

Few years later, that sh*t worth eight million

I can't wait to give this shit to my children

Y'all think it's bougie, I'm like, it's fine

But I'm tryin' to give you a million dollars worth of game for $9.99[33]"

"Y'all like Jay-Z, right?" Ms. Brown shouts smiling bobbing her head.

"Dang, Ms. B, you took it back with this one!" Jason cracks up.

I'm not gonna lie: It *is* kind of weird seeing Ms. Brown vibe to Jay-Z.

"Honestly Ms. Brown, Jay Z is old school. We like Cardi B and Ariana Grande," I answer.

The class agrees with me.

---

[33] Jay Z, "The Story of OJ," Track 2 on 4:44, Roc Nation, 2017, Tidal

"Nah, we gone, 'Count it up, count it up, count it up, count it. Can't take it when you die, but you can't live without it'. Now, J. Cole is the Goat!" Brandon shouts.

Brandon and Jason high-five each other. They *do* like J. Cole.

"Jay-Z is still dropping bombs though," Sean says.

"True, true," Brandon looks at Sean and nods his head.

"Well, if you guys want to be like Cole and Jay-Z, learn how to count it up."

"Ahhh," The class teases Ms. Brown.

I can't believe today is the last day of the club. I'm not going to lie, I am sad. I drop down in my chair, as the rest of the kids come into the classroom. I take out my phone, check my notifications on IG, and turn it on silent.

Ms. Brown turns off the music and stands up. She is smiling extra hard this time. I wonder who will be speaking today. I look at Jason and mouth the words: Something is up. He looks at me and smirks.

"Everyone, I have a special guest for you guys."

"Who is it?" Brandon asks.

Ms. Brown sits on the edge of her desk, folding her arms.

"Is it someone famous?" Sam, one of the newer kids, ask.

"Nope, it's me," Ms. Brown throws her hands in the air and starts milly whopping and reciting lyrics as if the music were still playing, "We talking about Credit today!"

"Okay, Ms. Brown!" Brandon yells and starts dancing with her. I can't help but laugh out loud. The whole class is #dead.

154

"Okay, okay, guys let's get down to it. Can anyone tell me what credit is?" Ms. Brown calms the class.

Ashley raises her hand. It is crazy to see Ashley speaking now; I have had two classes with her, she's no longer a turtle.

"Credit is when you have an agreement to borrow money now and agree to it pay it back at a later date, typically with interest."

"Exactly," Ms. Brown says. I look behind me. Ashley and I make eye contact. I smile at her, and she smiles back at me.

Ms. Brown pulls her hair back. "I need two volunteers to put this in action."

Brandon and Jason shoot their hands up.

Ms. Brown shakes her hand, "Nope, not you two."

Brandon protests and Jason shouts, "Come on."

I roll my eyes. They always have to do stuff together. I swear, these two are something else.

"Okay, guys anybody else want to volunteer, anybody," Ms. Brown scours the room, "Ashley what about you?" I look behind at Ashley again, her face is bright red.

"Okay," she squeaks.

"Well, come on up!" Ms. Brown points at me, "And Rebecca."

Ms. Brown hands us each a script.

"Okay," Ashley and I both say.

"Action." Ms. Brown claps.

Chapter 19: *Let Me Hold A 5*

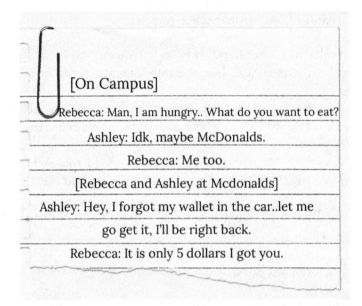

[On Campus]

Rebecca: Man, I am hungry.. What do you want to eat?

Ashley: Idk, maybe McDonalds.

Rebecca: Me too.

[Rebecca and Ashley at Mcdonalds]

Ashley: Hey, I forgot my wallet in the car..let me

go get it, I'll be right back.

Rebecca: It is only 5 dollars I got you.

"Okay, Rebecca and Ashley usually eat lunch together, but this time Ashley left her wallet behind," Ms. Brown explains. "Rebecca, in this case, if you gave your friend money, would you expect it back?"

"Nah, because I told her I got her."

"I would pay for her stuff," Hailey interjects. "But I would still expect her to pay me back, it is not like she doesn't have any money, she left her wallet in the car."

"Hmmm," Ms. Brown cups her chin. "I see your point Hailey, maybe Rebecca is being nice."

Ms. Brown tells us to continue.

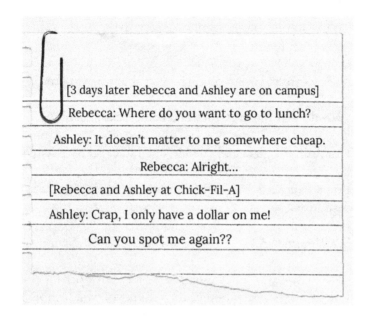

[3 days later Rebecca and Ashley are on campus]

Rebecca: Where do you want to go to lunch?

Ashley: It doesn't matter to me somewhere cheap.

Rebecca: Alright...

[Rebecca and Ashley at Chick-Fil-A]

Ashley: Crap, I only have a dollar on me!

Can you spot me again??

"Rebecca," Ms. Brown looks at me again.

"Last week, you gave Ashley money to buy her food and you didn't expect to be paid back. This week, she forgot again, are you still *inclined* to cover for her?"

"I would still cover her, if she paid me back the last time?"

"What if she didn't pay you back, would you cover her?"

"Well, I don't know, the first time I didn't think much about it. I wasn't expecting her to pay me back."

"What are your expectations now?"

"I would expect her to pay me back from here on out."

"Got it. Would you trust Ashley to borrow money from you again?"

"Hmmm… I think so."

"What if this same scenario keeps happening with Ashley's wallet?"

"I don't think so, I would feel like she is playing me."

"Would that mean Ashley is reliable or unreliable?"

Unreliable? I glance at Ashley, she looks pretty reliable to me.

I do a half shrug. "Uh…if she pays me back yes, she is reliable, if she doesn't then no."

Ms. Brown agrees. She gestures for us to sit down.

"This script was an example of how credit works. Lenders will give you money based on whether they think you will be able to pay it back. Make sense?"

Ms. Brown clears her throat, "The people who give you money are called lenders. Lenders can be banks, retail stores, finance and loan companies, credit card companies, etc. Unlike having money lent to you by a friend, if you don't pay these companies back, you can rack up fees, fall into debt, or worse, get your stuff repossessed."

Ms. Brown begins writing on the board:

How to Establish Credit

- **Open up a Bank Account / Savings Account**
- **Apply for a gas card or a department store card**
- **Apply for a secured card**

"Many of you have already started establishing credit by opening a bank account, again a banking account is a great first step."

Components of a FICO Score

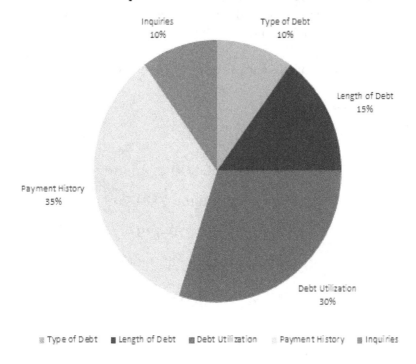

Inquiries
10%

Type of Debt
10%

Length of Debt
15%

Payment History
35%

Debt Utilization
30%

▦ Type of Debt　▪ Length of Debt　▪ Debt Utilization　Payment History　▪ Inquiries

34

"There are five components that determine your credit score: payment history, current level of indebtedness, types of credit used, length of credit history, and new credit accounts. This table shows the percentage each has on your score."

"Who decides your credit score?" Sean asks.

---

34 "Discover." Discover. Accessed September 13, 2019.
https://www.discover.com/credit-cards/help-center/faqs/free-fico.html#in-credit-score.

"Your credit score is determined by a credit score agency. Credit score agencies are called borrowers. One of the most popular scores is your FICO, created by Fair Isaac Corporation. Borrowers use the FICO score to assess credit risk. Lenders determine whether to extend credit to people or not."

"And what makes lenders give people credit?" I ask.

"I'm glad you asked."

☐ Exceptional-800 or higher

☐ Very Dependable-740-799

☐ Good Score- 670-739

☐ Some Approve- 580-669

☐ Risky- 579 & below

WHAT YOUR FICO
SCORE MEANS TO LENDERS

[35]

"So, the goal is to have 670 or higher?" Max asks.

"Good question," Ms. Brown says. "670 is good...but the higher your credit score, the better off you'll be."

"Take a look at these examples."

---

[35] "Card Benefits." Citi® Card Benefits - FICO® Score. Accessed September 13, 2019. https://www.cardbenefits.citi.com/Products/FICO-Score?cmp=7~1~64~1~042317~1~CKCHP~AddtlResources~InsightsTools.

Scenario 1

$400 PS4 Pro

Credit
8% APR

Min payment
2.25% ($9)

How long to pay off loan at minimum payment?

53 months (4.42 years)

How much will you pay after interest?

$475.97

Ms. Brown clears her throat, "A teenager decides to buy a PS4 Pro with his new credit card for $400. With good credit, and paying the minimum payment, he ended up spending a little over $475 over 4 years! Now, let's check out how the scenario plays out with a bad score," says Ms. Brown.

Scenario 2

$400 PS4 Pro

Credit
17.99% APR

Min payment
2.5% ($10)

How long to pay off loan at minimum payment?

62 months (5.17 years)

How much will you pay after interest?

$615.21

"What do you guys notice?

"The APR is almost twice as high, I say!"

"Right!" Ms. Brown explains, "if you don't have good credit, you will be more likely to pay higher interest rates. And if you only pay the minimum payment every month, it will take you longer to pay, causing interest to build. You will be paying more than what you paid initially."

Brandon shakes his head.

The class groans.

"We see, good credit is important, now let's discuss how to keep it that way," says Ms. Brown.

HOW TO
MAINTAIN A GOOD
CREDIT RATING

- ESTABLISH A GOOD CREDIT HISTORY
- NEVER MISS A PAYMENT AND MAKE PAYMENTS ON TIME
- USE CREDIT CARDS SPARINGLY
- STAY WITHIN THE LIMIT
- NO BALANCE TRANSFERS
- CHECK CREDIT REPORT REGULARLY

[36]

---

[36] Irby, LaToya. "Ways to Protect Your Credit Score." The Balance, December 17, 2018. https://www.thebalance.com/maintain-good-credit-score-960513.

"Maintaining good credit is vital, missed payments can cause your credit score to go down! It is very important you never miss a payment. If you miss a payment you will be charged a late fee. It is best to pay your bill in full. If you can't, pay as much as you can over the minimum payment."

"You should also stay away from balance transfers. Balance transfers are used by consumers who want to move their debt to a credit card in order to receive lower interest rates and fewer penalties. Although this is a great way to reduce the amount of interest you pay on your debt, your score will take a hit."

- Pay everything on time and as much as you can
- Don't go over the credit limit
- Credit report checks
- No transfers

Ms. Brown claps her hands, "Alright y'all, this is the last slide of *The Money Club*." Ms. Brown makes a sad face, we all groan.

"Wow, I have never seen you guys so sad!"

RISKS OF CREDIT

 Interest

Overspending

Debt

Identity theft

[37]

"The last topic about credit cards we need to know, is risk. Interest is the risk that you take by paying with credit instead of cash. Debt is the entire amount of money you owe to lenders. Another big risk when using credit cards is overspending, make sure you live within your means!" Ms. Brown takes a long sigh.

---

[37] Irby, LaToya. "The Dangers of Credit Card Debt and How to Avoid Them." The Balance, August 29, 2019. https://www.thebalance.com/dangers-of-credit-cards-960217.

"I have had trouble with overspending in the past. Be mindful when using credit cards, you are spending someone else's money; and you have to pay it back. You don't want to spend more than you can pay back. You have to be disciplined. Alright, last up is identity theft."

"Is that when someone steals your credit card?" someone asks.

"Not quite. Identity theft is when a person's identification, like their name, social security number, or account number is stolen," Ms. Brown states.

"Wow, this is wild," Sean says.

"It is! A person can steal your identity and rack up purchases on a bunch of cards."

"Does this happen a lot?"

"Well, it happens more often than you think. It is important to learn to manage and protect your accounts."

Ms. Brown clears her throat. "If it happens to you, you may have to spend extensive time closing accounts and opening new ones; it may cost you a lot of money and time to fix credit records; you may even be denied loans or jobs due to identity theft. The consequences can be serious." Ms. Brown frowns. "Researchers say past identity theft victims were not aware until one month after their identity was stolen."

"How do we protect ourselves from identity theft?" Ashley asks.

"Ashley, I am glad you asked. Write this down."

Ways to Prevent Identity Theft

- Use the security feature on your mobile phone

- Use a safe place to store personal information

- Create complex passwords and update your passwords every two-three months

- Don't share personal information such as your social security number, birth date, or account numbers with unknown people

- Check your account statements once a month

- Be careful with using public Wi-Fi - if using, turn on your privacy settings on your device

- Only give out your social security number if necessary

"Floor is open, any questions?" Ms. Brown asks.

"What if we have more than one credit card?"

"It's a good thing if you have multiple credit cards, it helps boost your score. But if you owe on multiple credit cards, pay off the one with higher interest rates first." Ms. Brown smiles. "Good question. Do you have any others?"

"I see commercials about free flights and stuff. Can I get free flights with a credit card?"

"Hahaha, some credit cards offer special offers like flight miles and grace periods, for example no interest for the first twelve months. I would take advantage of those offers whenever you can."

"Are there websites or apps we can use?" Ashley calls out.

"These are a few resources you can use to help with credit cards and money management."

Online Resources/ Credit Card Calculators

- **Square (app)**
- **Mint (app)**
- www.creditcards.com
- www.nerdwallet.com
- **Creditreport.com**

Ms. Brown has a huge grin on her face, "Well..." Ms. Brown looks at the time, "*The Money Club* is over."

"Aww man, this is the last day!" Brandon yells.

"The club went by fast," Max calls out. We all echo their sentiments.

"I know, but hey, now you can say you learned something in school, right Brandon?" Ms. Brown looks right at him.

We all laugh.

"Alright, guys...*The Money Club* is over."

The classroom breaks into chatter.

I hope *The Money Club* becomes a class. I think it's definitely something we need here. There *was* a finance class at the Academy, so boring. But this was different, actually fun.

I walk to my car with Jason.

"Hey, you want to come eat with us?" I shout at Brandon.

"Yeah, you paying?!" Brandon yells back.

I shake my head. These clowns.

"If I pay, you gotta promise to pay me back!" I yell.

"Bet."

"Let's go." I unlock my car doors.

Ms. Brown

Chapter 21: It Is The Little Things

It is finally Friday. My students rush out of class as the bell rings. I breathe a long sigh of relief. Today, was the last day to turn in the study guide. I stressed the importance of turning it in, but still, some students didn't. Once again, I am frustrated, but it is the weekend. I can let it go for now. The test is Tuesday, they better not turn it in late. I don't want to hear any complaints.

I grab 1st, 2nd, and 4th period's bins. Surprisingly, 4th period's bin is heavy. A huge grin spreads across my face. I am pretty sure the whole class turned it in; or at least, I hope they did. Most of my students from 4th period attended *The Money Club*. Even if it was for the extra credit, I am satisfied. I check my watch; I could grade papers real quick.

I have so much to do this weekend. My sister's bridal shower is Saturday, I have to help Mom, and I need to go grocery shopping...oh, what the heck - why not? I shut the door and get down to business; it won't take me long to knock out a good chunk of them. I need to find the answer key and get moving.

I clean off my desk, plop down in my chair and scan through 4th period's stack. My heart sinks. I don't see Brandon's name. I flip through them again: I see Thomas, Serena, Jason, Ashley, Sean, Rebecca, but no Brandon. This kid...hmmph. I shake my head. He did not miss a day of *The Money Club*. In class he was paying attention, writing notes...everything.

"So much for the real world, Brandon," I say out loud.

You can't save everybody, my dad would say. He is right. I grind my teeth. I have put so much energy into this class and now to *The Money Club*. I thought for sure, Brandon's study guide would be here, finished. I flip through the 1st and 2nd period bins to make sure it wasn't lost somewhere.

No such luck. I put on some music to focus. I take out the answer key and dive into the stack of papers. I get through seven packets before I hear a knock on the door.

"Come in," I say. It is probably Suzanne wanting to stop and eat or something.

"Hey... Ms. Brown?"

I look up. Brandon? He is in the doorway, he looks upset.

"Brandon. Hey, what is wrong?"

He looks at his sneakers.

"Are you alright?"

"Nothing is wrong, I wanted to know if I could talk to you for a minute...I would have talked to you after class but you know how it is..." Brandon rubs his hands together.

"Yeah, no problem. How are things?" I put the study guide packets to the side and take off my reading glasses.

"Things are good..."

Brandon fidgets. He jams his hands in his jacket. He makes eye contact with me then his eyes trail off.

"Are you sure you are okay?" I ask again.

Brandon cracks into a smile.

"Of course, Ms. Brown, I am always good," Brandon laughs mid-sentence. "I came here to…well, I came to apologize."

I raise my eyebrows. Brandon has never apologized to me, *ever*. He hasn't even said "My bad" to me.

174

"Brandon, you don't-"

"Nah," Brandon interrupts me. "...I gave you a hard time about this study guide, but I don't want to fail, you know? I have been stressed, and I felt bad about being disrespectful."

For Brandon to say sorry...it means a lot to me. I don't come across apologies often here - maybe from parents but not from kids.

"Thank you, Brandon, for the apology, I appreciate it," I smile really wide.

Brandon begins walking towards the door and turns around.

"You know what, Ms. Brown?"

"Yeah?"

"College isn't for me, but I'm going to get my associates degree and help my uncle run his business; and guess what? I opened up a bank account with Mrs. Lawrence last week!"

"Well, good for you Brandon." I turn back to my desk to finish grading. Brandon drops a tattered packet of paper on my desk next to the 4th period bins.

"I did my study guide, no cheating or nothing."

I laugh out loud. Brandon laughs, too.

"Told you, I ain't no joke," Brandon struts out the classroom and throws up the peace sign.

"Hi, Ms. Brown," Jason's head peeks through the door. "You got my study guide, right?"

"Yes, I have yours, Jason."

"Mine too?" Rebecca's head appears underneath Jason's.

"You kids crack me up."

"We got to keep you on your toes, Ms. B!" Brandon exclaims.

They laugh and close the door. I shake my head in disbelief. Wow, just wow. I sit back in my chair and relish the moment. Brandon. Brandon Anderson apologized to me. *Me.* A teacher. Wow. I close my laptop unable to continue working. It is Friday, why am I still grading tests?! I chuckle to myself. I need to get home and give myself a toast. I reach into my purse to grab my keys.

"Ms. Brown is leaving early today, y'all," I shout out to the empty classroom. I walk out of my class, with my head held high, my heels clicking, and the biggest smile across my face.

I DID THAT.

$ $ $ $ $ $

After the club came to an end, I was overwhelmed with positive feedback from students, my peers, and especially Principal Matthews. Even Mr. Davis came by to apologize the next week!

I had no idea how much impact *The Money Club* would have at Lakewood High School. The following weeks, I had so many parents request me to start up the club again. I got approved to hold camps in the summer! And I already have forty kids signed up.

I am thrilled to say *The Money Club* will expand into a non-profit. I know it is weird to say, but Brandon's outburst is the reason behind *The Money Club*. His outburst fueled me to go above and beyond - I tried something different and I found my purpose.

Teaching is my passion, but I questioned whether teaching high school math was fulfilling. It is hard teaching; teachers have the toughest job in America. We are literally responsible for the success of the next generation. And we get nothing in return!

I can't tell you how many times I thought about quitting or how many times I felt unsure...I wanted to make a difference, I felt I was capable but never knew I could actually do it. My job as a math teacher is to help students pass, so they can graduate. That is it. I can't tell you how many other subjects are taught the same way. Sticking to the curriculum has cost teachers and students their value.

Kids aren't learning. They are left behind. It is sad. I do believe kids want to learn but their passion for learning is not there. We can't blame social media and smartphones for students' lack of engagement; instantaneous information has made us lazy as well. As a teacher, I feel I am always rushing - filling them up with busy work.

If we want to prepare students for real-world success, teaching kids finances along with other required courses is where we need to begin. I know I am not a financial advisor: I'm a woman whose passion is teaching kids. Teaching kids personal finances in school is the key. Managing and budgeting money will teach students real-world applications they can use beyond graduation. We don't have to get rid of math. We need to change our approach to it.

In *The Money Club*, I saw students paying attention. I witnessed them writing notes and checking over their notes carefully - even when we covered the most boring parts of finances - their eyes were glued to the subject at hand. When was the last time a high school math teacher had everyone in class pay attention? If you know when, please let me know.

If you don't believe me that finances are the answer, consider this: the student loan debt is in the trillions, many people are living pay-check to pay-check. Even people who make tons of money are struggling with finances. It affects us all. We need financial education at an early age before we go to college. In school, with passionate teachers who not only teach personal finances but who believe in its empowerment.

Not every child has access to resources to learn financial education and that is where schools come in - we can bridge the gap. Think how much better the world would be if people were financially educated and empowered? It could boost employment, eliminate debt, and help marriages stay together.

Both parents and schools are responsible for teaching financial literacy, but schools bear the brunt.

Wrestling with this question is tough. Some may say I shouldn't answer because I come from a privileged background - I acknowledge that I was blessed growing up. My dad ran his own business. I remember when I was two-feet-nothing, my dad would quiz my sister and I on stock symbols. As kids, we knew what it meant for the stock market to be "bullish" or "bearish"! My dad taught me. He saw the importance in educating us in financial literacy.

To say it is the parents' job to teach kids about money would be wrong. Many parents aren't financially stable, nor do they have the resources to teach their children. Financial illiteracy is a generational curse. The only way to break the curse is for the community and the school systems to step in.

Financial literacy is something everyone needs to learn and since many Americans are burdened with expenses, it is our job (educational institutions) to teach students personal finances.

My duty as a teacher is to ensure my students learn what they need to, pass down my knowledge from what I have learned from my life experiences, and help them become successful. I realized during the club, teaching is more than what I thought it was - teaching is a calling, and your calling is for life. Teaching doesn't stop in the classroom.

In terms of financial literacy; it used to be seen as a parent's responsibility, but more importantly, it is the community's. It takes a village. The school is the community, the school is the village.

What about the parents?

I have come to realize socio-economic status can influence the opportunities and privileges available to a community. Financial literacy is a privilege these days. How can people from less-than-privileged backgrounds teach kids the foundations and principles of money? How can a parent teach a child about opening a bank account if they have never had one?

How can people from those less-than-privileged backgrounds have the right knowledge for opening a bank account, drafting and sticking with a budget, getting and paying off a credit card, and eventually investing, paying off student loans, buying a house, or, finally, saving for retirement? Without the proper knowledge, they can be very easily taken advantage of. The real world *will* take advantage of them. I know this, and I still couldn't give myself a clear answer to my own question. Again, my brain asked me:

Is it the parents? In my case, my parents taught me. However, many parents are not equipped with this knowledge and aren't able to teach their children. Is it schools? Teachers already have too much on their hands.

I believe in my heart, schools need to be teaching financial literacy, but many states across the U.S. don't have mandated requirements for students to learn basic economics before graduating. When these kids get into the 'real world', they struggle. I find many high schools across the country place an importance on athletics and not education.

When kids are athletically gifted, especially in poverty-stricken environments, parents and teachers think their child will make it to the big leagues. In most sports, less than two percent of college athletes will go pro[38]; the system of our inner-city schools, especially within athletics, is setting these kids up for failure. The allure of fast money is smoke and mirrors, and when the smoke clears and reality sets in - which it does more times than not - and even when kids make it to the league, they struggle with their money and can still end up broke. I asked myself this:

Are we preparing students and student athletes for their desired workforce?

No, we aren't. When I answered this part, it became clear to me, I needed to create this change. It became crystal clear. I had to teach my students what is necessary to thrive in the world. After the Money Club was over, I made it my business to expand *The Money Club*. I spoke to my family and especially my dad about what I wanted to do.

After speaking to my family members and close friends, they encouraged me to start FACTS for Youth. FACTS is a non-profit organization dedicated to teaching student-athletes financial literacy.

Coming from an athletic background, my primary focus was on high school-aged athletes. I wanted athletes to realize they were more than muscles and a ball. I wanted them to know even if they didn't make it to the professional league, they could still be successful. For the students who do make it, I want them to know financial literacy (money management) will prevent them from going broke. It is crazy to think a professional athlete may go broke soon after they retire[39].

At first, my heart was dead set on focusing on athletes. I thought athletes needed it the most, but when I went out to schools in Robeson and Scotland counties, my mind changed. I met with kids who were worried about paying for college. I spoke with students who

---

[38] Rpowell. "Estimated Probability of Competing in Professional Athletics." NCAA.org - The Official Site of the NCAA, April 9, 2019. http://www.ncaa.org/about/resources/research/estimated-probability-competing-professional-athletics.

[39] Brooks, Rodney. "Why Do so Many Pros Go Broke?" The Undefeated. The Undefeated, March 28, 2017. https://theundefeated.com/features/why-do-so-many-pros-go-broke/.

wanted to learn how to budget and save for their family. I also met students who needed to be a financial resource for their siblings and parents. As I brought Facts to these communities, my heart and FACTS grew.

Students from every background need financial education. In fact, we all need it. If we want our future to be brighter, early education is a must.

When I saw what FACTS was doing and what FACTS could do, I knew I was doing the right thing. FACTS has changed my life and I am hoping it will change those who I come in contact with.

I want to leave you with this: finances do not have to be a burden because financial literacy is the solution!

Connect with Jasmine:

Instagram: @thejasmineamber | @_factsforyouth

Twitter: @_factsforyouth

Facebook: @factsforyouthnc

Email: info@factsforyouth.com

Website: www.factsforyouth.com

Free Resources

About.com: Basic monthly budget worksheet.

Bankrate.com: Great resource for rates and financial calculators.

Clark Howard: A good resource for general financial topics. Also a good daily radio show.

College Board: A student loan calculator from The College Board.

Consumer Credit Counseling Services: Reduce debt through debt relief.

Cost of Driving: a website that helps students investigate the full cost of owning and safely operating a car. An interactive calculator introduces students to comparison shopping for a car and payment options.

Debt.org: Learn to acquire, manage, and pay back different types of financial aid and student loan debt.

Dollar Sense: A budgeting game for middle and high school students.

Everfi Venture- Entrepreneurial Expedition: Curriculum designed to teach students to think entrepreneurially. Students develop a personalized plan for their own business, including financing, marketing, and market research, along with a roadmap for academic and career success.

Financial Entertainment: Helps consumers learn how to better manage money.

Finance In The Classroom: A comprehensive online resource that brings teachers, parents and community together to provide financial education to students.

Free Annual Credit Report: Free site to review your credit report.

Ignitespot: Information for budgeting and accounting, no matter your age.

Invest in What's Next: Free, online course that helps students evaluate their choices for one of the biggest decisions they'll face-what path to pursue after high school.

Investor.gov: An online resource to help you learn how to make sound investment decisions and avoid fraud.

Life Happens: Helps you easily understand insurance needs.

Mint.com : Great for budgeting, brings all your money in one place.

Money Matters: Make it Count: Promotes financial responsibility and independence for students age 13-18 by building money management skills.

Money Teach: an online resource center for personal finance educators to find lesson plans, course guides and other materials for a personal finance course.

MyMoney.gov: the federal government's website dedicated to helping Americans understand more about their money -- how to save it, invest it, manage it.

Next Gen Personal Finance (NGPF): A free, online library of 1500+ personal finance resources.

Practical Money Skills: Practical Money Skills from the NFLPA.

Securities Exchange Commission: Tips on investing and saving for students.

Show Me The Future: A game and simulation designed for students age 12-20. The game helps players understand concepts such as cost of living, budgeting, wants and needs, financial planning, career goals, and the value of higher education.

Simple Tuition: Great way to compare student loans

Student Loan Calculator: How long will it take to pay off my student loan? Bankrate's Student Loan Calculator can help students and their families find the answer.

The Mint: An online guide for teenagers, families and teachers to designed to help children become money smart.

WalletWise: A collection of free online courses designed to help students build healthy personal finance habits and make sound financial decisions that work with their lifestyle and support their goals.

We Need to Talk College: An online multimedia guide that helps families navigate the college process—from having the initial conversation, to decoding financial aid, to choosing the right school for the students' needs.